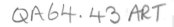

Rapid Evolutionary Development

WILEY SERIES IN
SOFTWARE ENGINEERING PRACTICE

SERIES EDITORS:

Patrick A.V. Hall, The Open University, UK
Martyn A. Ould, Praxis Systems plc, UK
William E. Riddle, Software Design & Analysis, Inc., USA

Fletcher J. Buckley • Implementing Software Engineering Practices

John J. Marciniak and Donald J. Reifer • Software Acquisition Management

John S. Hares • SSADM for the Advanced Practitioner

Martyn A. Ould • Strategies for Software Engineering: The Management of Risk and Quality

David P. Youll • Making Software Development Visible: Effective Project Control

Charles P. Hollocker • Software Reviews and Audits Handbook

David Whitgift • Software Configuration Management: Methods & Tools

John S. Hares • Information Engineering for the Advanced Practitioner

Robert L. Baber • Error Free Programming

H. Ronald Berlack • Software Configuration Management

Ken Shumate and Marilyn Keller • Software Specification & Design: A Disciplined Approach for Real-Time Systems

L. Jay Arthur • Rapid Evolutionary Development: Requirements, Prototyping, & Software Creation

Michael Dyer • The Cleanroom Approach to Quality Software Development

Rapid Evolutionary Development

Requirements, Prototyping &
Software Creation

LOWELL JAY ARTHUR

John Wiley & Sons, Inc.
New York / Chichester / Brisbane / Toronto / Singapore

Copyright © 1992 by John Wiley & Sons, Inc.

All rights reserved. Published simultaneously in Canada.

Reproduction or translation of any part of this work beyond that permitted
by section 107 or 108 of the 1976 United States Copyright Act without the
permission of the copyright owner is unlawful. Requests for permission
or further information should be addressed to the Permission Department,
John Wiley & Sons, Inc.

This publication is designed to provide accurate and authoratative information
in regard to the subject matter covered. It is sold with the understanding
that the publisher is not engaged in rendering legal, accounting, or other
professional service. If legal or other expert assistance is required,
the services of a competent professional person should be sought. *From a
Declaration of Principles jointly adopted by a Committee of the
American Bar Association and a Commmittee of Publishers.*

Library of Congress Cataloging-in-Publication Data

Arthur, Lowell Jay. 1951–
     Rapid evolutionary development : requirements, prototyping &
software creation / L. Jay Arthur.
          p.   cm.
     Includes bibliographical references.
     ISBN 0–471–53633–4
     1. Computer software—Development.   I. Title.
QA76.76.D4A78 1991
005.1—dc20   91–16670

Printed in the United States of America
10 9 8 7 6 5 4 3 2 1

*A tree that can fill the span
of a man's arms
grows from a downy tip;*

*A terrace nine stories high
rises from handfuls of earth*

*A journey of a thousand miles
starts from beneath one's feet.*

Lao-tzu

CONTENTS

Human artistry has evolved from canvases of stone to modern computer graphics. The process of software development, although still young, is as rigid and slow to change as early cave drawings. To survive and thrive in the information era, we must evolve to a new level of artistry and ability—rapid evolutionary development.

Courtesy of the Denver Museum of Natural History.

More than 20 years have passed while software development methodology has evolved to little more than a black art.

— Ted G. Lewis and Paul W. Oman

The amount of money spent on software grows at a rate of approximately 12 percent per year (Humphrey 1988). If we look closely at the software development and maintenance processes currently in use, it is obvious to most software practitioners that there must be a better way. External *and* internal customers are demanding faster solutions to increasingly complex problems. And then, once the solution is delivered, there has to be a way to keep it in line with changes in the environment, marketplace, and the company itself. Failure to do so means extinction for the system and sometimes the company. We need a "better way" to meet the need for rapid technical solutions to business problems that fits the way people work, not the way technology has forced them to work in the past, but a way that draws on what we already know—the current state of the art. We need a way that isn't too clever, a way that anyone can understand. That is what this book is all about.

Let's begin by taking a historical journey through science. Galileo looked into the heavens and, based on what he observed, deduced that the Earth moved around the sun, not the other way around. Charles Darwin traveled around the world gathering information about life on planet Earth and *then* he looked for a concept that fit the data he found. Albert Einstein, using data gathered about the universe that didn't fit the existing model, began to ask himself what concept would fit the available data. From this he developed the theory of relativity. Similarly, while studying scientific revolutions, Thomas Kuhn discovered that all great revelations came from scientists who synthesized models of the world that fit the available data.

And that is what I have done in this book. Based on 20 years of experience and observation, I have developed a model that fits the way software is successfully produced and it will surprise and delight you in many ways as you begin to learn its way.

This book has two basic premises:

1. A complex system that works *evolves* from a simple system that works via rapid prototyping and software evolution.
2. A complex system designed from scratch *never works* and *cannot be patched up* to make it work (specification, large-scale development, and maintenance). You have to start over, beginning with a simple, working system (prototyping and evolutionary development).

However, software development as we know it has followed two main paradigms—construction and manufacturing:

- Construction: Software can be specified and constructed in its final, fully functioning form. This is a high-risk endeavor. All too often, the delivered system does not provide what the user wants, but you cannot observe this until the system is delivered. By then, it is too late to do anything about it. The construction paradigm is the major reason that so many customers are dissatisfied and maintenance is considered such a lowly position.

- Manufacturing: Software can be prespecified and a manufacturing line developed to mass produce software. Software, however, is not a mass-produced item; it is a custom product in most instances.

In this book, we'll look at a slightly different paradigm of software development and maintenance. I will suggest to you that software doesn't *build*, it *grows* and *evolves*. The paradigm of software evolution suggests that software must grow and evolve from simple "life forms" into more complex and advanced life forms. These simple life forms (e.g., cells, data, modules) are the building blocks of larger organisms or systems.

Rapid prototyping, set in the context of rapid evolutionary development, is the only way that software can be created and grown into successful systems in short time frames. The construction paradigm will always take longer and cost more because we simply don't have the information necessary to build the complete system initially. With rapid evolutionary development we can learn and grow along with the system as it evolves.

Early software development was characterized by the evolutionary, build a little, implement a little philosophy. Then someone grabbed hold of the construction-manufacturing paradigm which suggests that we can layout an architecture, design the system, and construct it. Experience has shown that this is a painful and expensive way to develop dinosaurs. We forgot that thousands of years of evolution in building have led from the simple mud hut to skyscrapers. Plumbing wasn't common in homes until the 1930s. Architecture is still evolving, but it still relies on a few basic shapes—box, sphere, and cylinder. Software still relies on the *waterfall* model and spaghetti metaphor. All we get are species of software on the edge of extinction.

Applications of the past saw themselves as islands, unrelated to the other systems around them. Like nature, however, every system is part of the total environment—dependent on everything around it. Like the food chain in the earth's ecosystem, there is an information chain that feeds the computer networks and ultimately the human brain's enormous appetite for knowledge and wisdom. Today we hear a little word called *integration*, but we have few ideas about how to achieve it.

To understand evolutionary development, software engineers need to model our greatest teacher—nature. A giant oak does not spring forth fully formed from a tiny seed and neither do software systems. Like a giant oak, software can begin from a tiny seed, a concept. Then as a tiny plant, the system can extend a tap root into the corporate data, and a tender stalk and a few leaves to catch the sun. As the sun and the rain nurture it from above, the earth nourishes it from below. Carefully tended, it can grow into a great system that will bear fruit for everyone and we need to remember that oak trees did not spring forth in their current form. Birds, plants, animals, and fish evolved based on the nature of their environment—wind, earth, or water. Software engineers seem to deal mainly with the fourth element of the universe—fire—as in firefighting, damage control, and so on.

Our past focus on technology has not delivered its promised orders of magnitude improvement in productivity or quality. The structured methodologies that we've followed have locked us into a stiff and unbending discipline that alientates our customer.

We need to shift from the old models of software development and maintenance—construction and manufacturing—to a new, more resourceful model of software development—software evolution. Rapid evolutionary development, the creation portion of software evolution, makes our customers our partners. This book will show a software engineer how to plant, grow, and evolve small systems into large ones rapidly, with a high degree of customer involvement and success.

Evolutionary development is all around us.

1. Existing systems (i.e., in maintenance) are *evolutionary prototypes* (i.e., they are evolving to meet business needs. This makes software maintenance an "evolutionary" development process). Unfortunately, the "quick fix" mentality of most maintenance shops tend to mutate software rather than evolve it. How do we keep software on the evolutionary path?

   Many people are trying to develop replacement systems by sending people off into a room for six weeks to develop requirements when they already have a working prototype running every day in the field. Why not use the knowledge embedded in these systems?

2. Versioning, in the development process, is the same as evolutionary development, but the names have been changed to help manage user expectations and discourage management meddling.

3. Continuous changes to the requirements during development are evolutionary changes at work. Since we can't fully prespecify a system's requirements, they must change and grow during the development process. That is why rapid prototyping is so exciting; it is a living, learning, and growing experience. Why freeze requirements when they can be allowed to expand?

4. Software enhancements, especially in the first two years of a system's life, are due to massive flaws in the original requirements and design. Vast efforts are under way in many software maintenance projects today to correct the genetic flaws in the systems delivered only yesterday. Evolution at its finest!

This book will focus on the four keys to productivity and quality:

1. The people
2. The evolutionary process they use
3. The tools that support the process
4. And the evolutionary means to grow the development environment

People—customers and developers alike—are the key to project success and continuous improvement. Systems consist of not only software, but the people, training, documentation, and hardware that make it all work—a meta-system or ecosystem that includes all aspects of the system.

The process of rapid evolutionary development is widely known: God created the heavens and the earth in six days—the prototype. Hundreds of millions of years of evolution were required to get it to the point it is now.

There are two common forms of prototypes: *throw-away* prototypes that are a result of our "construction and manufacturing" paradigm and *evolutionary* prototypes that are the result of the software evolution paradigm. The latter, suggests Brooks and Mills (Brooks 1988), is the way to create systems. "Software should be grown by incremental development. Prototyping lends itself to early prototypes. Each added function and new provision for more complex data or circumstances grows *organically* out of what is already there. Enthusiasm jumps when there is a running system, even a simple one. Teams can *grow* more complex entities in four months than they can *build*." Prototyping is not only the requirements definition strategy for the 1990s, it is the foundation for evolutionary software development in the 1990s.

Prototyping involves the client in the day-to-day development and evolution of the required system. Unfortunately, software developers have not been listening to the voice of their customer. Customers don't want a prototype that demonstrates what they want—they want one they can *use*. Typically, 20 percent of the application will deliver 80 percent of the required functionality—a simple system that works. This 20 percent should be the focus of the initial prototyping process. Ensuing work will evolve the prototype into the desired product.

Rapid prototyping has many advantages. It:

- Is simple to do
- Provides value in a short time frame
- Allows early, easy wins that establish "creeping customer commitment"
- Lowers risk — projects can be canceled at any time; software battles are fought every day and an estimated 25 percent of all software projects are canceled for one reason or another
- Allows software engineers and clients to learn as they go; many things you need to know to develop a system are unknown and unknowable in the beginning

The disadvantages of rapid prototyping are really advantages in disguise. Rapid prototyping is only as useful as the product it produces:

- A well-built system is its own heaven; a poorly built one is its own hell. Rapid evolutionary development requires software engineers to be the keepers of the holy vision and the technology that implements it. Otherwise, the process will produce the same old junk we've always delivered. The system has to be implemented using the best-known, most-effective techniques. Prototypers must keep the overall *ecology* of the meta-system in mind at all times. While working in the present, prototypers must have a strong sense of how their work will impact the future. Prototyping is not the place to be sloppy. It is the place to set the course and direction for system's life span.
- The prototype must focus on and deliver the qualities required in the resulting system—flexibility, maintainability, and reusability.

Before, during, and after prototyping comes the complex part—managing user expectations. The prototype can often be constructed quickly, but adding in the other 80 percent of the system that provides the other 20 percent of the benefit requires a structured evolutionary process, like the one I described in *Software Evolution—The Software Maintenance Challenge* (1988). It doesn't take as much effort to create a prototype that you can demonstrate, but it can take a lot more effort to make a product that is strong enough to withstand the forces of nature that will assault it once it is delivered into production.

With the rapid evolutionary development methodology firmly in hand, people should choose their weapons to match the war, not choose a bunch of weapons and then run around looking for a war that matches their tools.

Tools and technology *support* rapid prototyping, evolutionary development, and continuous quality improvement. *Any tool kit will work.* I've often used whatever tools were handy to dig into the needs of the user. Of course, I occasionally had to abandon whole technologies when they wouldn't work or support evolution. That's okay—nature has abandoned many evolutionary failures, but it didn't despair; it just tried a new, improved life form. Like life, some tool kits will be better for one type of problem than they will be for another. Choosing the right tool to match the problem is better than trying to fit the problem to the tool.

The software creation process must continuously evolve to do a better job each time. This involves using quality improvement and the PDCA (plan, do, check, act) process for continuous improvement. The absence of this simple technique has held software development to the minimal productivity and quality gains of the 1970s and 1980s. Why has hardware seen 35 percent improvement per year? In large part, this improvement is due to the embedded culture of PDCA used in manufacturing.

Ultimately, we need to be able to deliver robust functionality (but not full functionality) in nine months with nine people. When Brooks said that "bearing a child takes nine months, no matter how many women are assigned" (1975), he didn't know how right he was. Monolithic development simply does not support thriving on chaos in the 1990s. Market windows open and close too rapidly. Businesses that adopt an evolutionary strategy of software development will survive and thrive. Those who do not will become dinosaurs of the 20th century. Which does your company want to be?

In this book I will invite you to examine the way you view software development and maintenance, and about what is possible in the realms of productivity and quality. By the time you finish reading Chapter 1, you will be aware of the possibilities involved in a new paradigm of software development and maintenance—software evolution. And by the time you finish the book, you will have the tools you need to master rapid evolutionary development. Together with my other book on software maintenance (Arthur 1988), you will be well on your way to software mastery.

By the time an industry growing rapidly has doubled in volume, the way it perceives and services its market is likely to have become inappropriate.
— *Peter E. Drucker*

The rapid growth of the software industry has left little time for examination and alteration of its childhood beliefs, attitudes, and behaviors. The future suggests that even more rapid growth is in store in the next decade. Without a software model that facilitates this growth, such a change could indeed be painful.

Global markets and continuous changes in the business environment demand rapid solutions to business problems. The strength of a company's information systems will be a source of strength or costly mismanagement. Well-managed and continuously improved information systems will serve as a strategic thrust for competitive firms of the 1990s. Poorly managed information systems will lead to disaster.

Aligning business and information systems and structures will be the key competitive weapon of the 1990s. This can only be achieved through flexibility inherent in a new approach to software development and maintenance—software evolution. Integrated methods and tools for software creation and evolution will be the foundation of business success.

The strategic advantage of information will be exploited in this decade in ways that can only be imagined. A key reason for the power of information systems is the shift from using information to guide tactical business activities to one of using information to identify new markets and slaughter competitors in existing markets. Continuous evolution of information will be the key competitive weapon that will determine the survivors in the next millenium.

The convergence of new and existing methodologies and technologies now makes it possible to dramatically change our paradigms of software development and maintenance. Where once software developers relied on the "construction" paradigm which could only build inflexible vertical systems slowly and at great expense, waste, and rework, software creationists and evolutionists can now grow flexible, living, breathing, changing technology solutions at rates not previously imaginable.

CHAPTER 1

Software Evolution

We are all a miracle of creation. After nine months of incubation, a child arrives in the world where he or she can begin to increase life's experience and growth. From the moment we are born, we begin to learn, to grow, and to change. In early childhood, our parents care for us. We depend on them for guidance, nurturing, and direction. Then other teachers begin to expand our knowledge and abilities. During adolescence, we develop an independence that is essential to our continued growth. Finally, we leave the family and begin our adulthood—independence from and interdependence with other people.

Such has been my experience with successful software projects. The user or customer comes together with the information systems (IS) personnel to begin a rather awkward, arranged marriage. Together, they begin the creation of a family. At the moment of *concept*-ion, the two forces meet and begin the prototyping process, which through mitosis and differentiation, grows the concept into a fetal system that eventually acquires enough capabilities to be delivered into production. It is not, however, a fully mature, adult system. In its infancy, the system requires routine feeding, care and maintenance, and an almost daily change of diapers. It gets sick occasionally and needs to be carried for months, if not years, to allow its continued growth. Then, one day, it begins to walk, talk, and feed itself. At this point, other departments develop an interest in its future and growth. They begin to teach it new things. It grows into adolescence and suddenly its hormones begin to race. It develops skin conditions and a host of related phenomena. Finally, it graduates from school and leaves the family. The system, which is used to working alone, begins to interact with other systems and departments. Often, like people, it discovers it has no skills to do so. The physically mature system must learn how to grow and evolve, which is not always a simple process.

> *A new scientific truth does not triumph by convincing its opponents and making them see the light, but rather because its opponents eventually die, and a new generation grows up that is familiar with it.*
>
> — *Max Planck*

You are probably wondering what evolution and Darwin's theory have to do with software and how they relate to prototyping and software creation. Darwin's theory highlights three factors: random genetic variation, natural selection (survival of the fittest), and gradual changes accumulated over a long period of time, punctuated by brief periods of rapid change. To understand how rapid prototyping fits into this scheme of development, you have to understand the overall process that encompasses it and brings forth its true value—Software Evolution.

Many people have asked me: What is Software Evolution? To begin with, the word "evolution" means unfolding. Software is a unique life form that unfolds over time. Software Evolution, therefore, is a new way of looking at software development and maintenance that follows the natural processes of software creation, growth, and evolution.

> *Every revolution was first a thought in one man's mind; and when the same thought occurs to another man, it is the key to that era.*
>
> — *Emerson*

The concept of software evolution is not new; the first references appeared in 1975 (Belady & Lehman 1976) and more recently in 1989 (Luqi 1989). Oddly enough, it simply didn't get enough recognition, which is often the case with new paradigms. One reason for this failure to understand this new paradigm is found in Drucker (1986). In *Innovations and Entrepreneurship*, Drucker describes the key characteristics of "knowledge-based innovations." The first characteristic is the 25–35 year time span required to make the shift from one paradigm to another. Penicillin was discovered in the mid-1920s and rammed into development during World War II. The essential knowledge to build a computer was available in 1918, but not developed until 1946.

The second characteristic of knowledge-based innovations ''is that they are almost never based on one factor but on the convergence of several different kinds of knowledge, not all of them scientific or technological.'' The essential knowledge required for rapid creation and evolution of software has existed for at least 15 years, but has not been brought together. The knowledge required is not all technological, as you will discover; much of the knowledge is sociological and psychological. This book will explore in detail all of the knowledge required to master Software Evolution.

The mounting information crisis and global competition of the 1990s demand that this new paradigm enter the mainstream of software if we are to maintain a worldwide competitive advantage. Software Evolution cannot wait another 10 to 20 years. The marketplace will not stand for the common delays and cost overruns of the current paradigm. There simply isn't time.

SOFTWARE METAPHORS

The Fixed Wheel of Tradition only maintains itself. When this happens there are no new Gifts, and the People are Hungry. A Blind Wheel of endless tradition is always destined to destroy itself.

— *Hyemeyohsts Storm*

George Lakoff, a linguist at the University of Chicago, looked into how we use language to describe our experience (Lakoff & Johnson 1980). What he discovered is fascinating: rather than making metaphors that match our experience, *we make our experience match our metaphor.* That is, people and organizations tend to live in ways that match their dominant metaphor. So what is a metaphor?

Consider the metaphor that *business is war.* If we operate using this metaphor, then we can attack a market, or defend our position. Using this metaphor, we want to *kill* the competition. If we think of business as sport, instead, then we *seek* skillful opponents to test our skills and provide proof of our superiority. In business as war, if we lose, we die. In business as sport, we expect to lose occasionally because it will help us develop a winning team.

The metaphor we choose for software development and maintenance will direct and unify the overall software effort. The metaphor that allows us to understand software in one way will necessarily hide other aspects of the concept. Metaphors for software development should embody the:

- Desired vision for software development and maintenance
- Values and criteria
- Beliefs and culture

The reigning paradigm of software development and maintenance is based entirely on the metaphors of *construction* or *manufacturing*. Thinking about software in terms of construction suggests that we can *build* large systems from user's requirements that are often shaky at best. The construction paradigm insists that we have *complete knowledge* of requirements and technology, that we have fixed stages with specific, defect-free products, and no unresolved issues. Experience has shown that this paradigm is the road to ruin—excessive cost and schedule overruns, employee burnout, and outright customer mutiny. System construction would work well if the requirements were both well known and static, neither of which is true of information systems.

The construction paradigm is very linear—one phase after another—using the "waterfall" model. Most of the time, programmers and analysts feel more like salmon swimming against the flow, not with it. This one-way flow increases the possibility of transmitting an error from one stage to the next with each rigid step we take. Think about the waterfall metaphor: We should cascade easily and effortlessly to a solution; instead we rush headlong toward a deadline, unwilling to take time to do it right the first time. The waterfall metaphor makes swimming back up to improve a previous stage almost impossible. Most projects become like a trip over Niagara Falls, a frightening one-way trip that crashes onto the rocks below with no room or ability to retrace our steps if there appears to be an easier way to the solution. The waterfall metaphor also prevents us from stopping projects. It seems that once a project begins, no matter how big it gets or how ridiculous it becomes, it has to go forward to the bitter end.

The worn-out phrase "Build it right the first time" has proven to be an impossible goal, because it rests on the unstable foundation of the construction paradigm and the waterfall metaphor. The construction paradigm suffers from several problems:

- Unpredictable schedules
- Unpredictable costs
- High maintenance costs
- Short system life (crib death, infanticide, and genetic disorders)

Here is the truth about making a plan: It never works. If, however, you do make
a plan, the chances of getting what you want significantly increase.
— John-Roger and Peter McWilliams

Why is it impossible to "build it right the first time"? Software has
proven to be anything but soft. Software should be flexible. Again, the
construction paradigm is at the heart of the problem. Think of the products
of construction. Think about all of the buildings you see every day. Are
they flexible or rigid, bending or stiff? Are they easily connected to the
other buildings around them? Are they easy to re-engineer or restructure?

The answer is *no!*

The construction paradigm pulls the heart out of the prototyping process
as well. If you think about it, most architects construct three-dimensional
representations of the final building. They draw lots of diagrams and show
many pictures, but the prototype is only a mock version that is never used.
Its sole function is to get funding to build the final product! Then the
"real" work begins and several years later a structure exists that people
can begin using.

The other reigning metaphor of software production is the manufacturing metaphor. The manufacturing metaphor resigns people to routine jobs
that produce identical widgets day in and day out. The requirements and
design are fixed before production begins. Manufacturing implies either a
human-intensive process or one that relies on robots. It is no wonder that
with the human-intensive activities required to develop software that IS
departments have jumped to buy CASE tools and application generators to
automate the assembly line process. Unfortunately, the software factory
seems to be incapable of rolling out even the simplest Model T, let alone a
model with hundreds of available options. Current software factories are
more like some automobile assembly lines where workers hand tool every
part of a very expensive car. Are these handcrafted systems easy to evolve
or grow?

Again the answer is *no!*

The stiff and unbending is the discipline of death
The gentle and yielding is the discipline of life
— The Tao Te Ching

Manufacturing often requires a variety of prototypes before the assembly line can be set up. Prototypes range from clay models of cars or
airplanes to actual working versions. These prototypes are still viewed as
interim products that need to exist before the actual work of setting up the
assembly line and staffing the plant to get production underway can be

implemented. Software development is not mass production; it's mass *customization*—creating unique, but similar systems that meet the varying needs of customers. That's why they are called customers, not producers or some other ridiculous name.

The construction and manufacturing paradigms also suggest that, like most buildings or manufactured goods, they will require maintenance. Using these metaphors, we expect software to require maintenance. Compare this to living organisms which tend to have their own defenses and regenerative or restorative abilities. If you scratch yourself, your body knows how to heal itself and it does. Only in extreme cases do living systems need doctors, the mechanics of the human body, to fix them. Even now, more people and doctors are turning to "wellness" as a way of preventing disease and the need for surgery or drugs. Software can be created with wellness in mind to prevent much of the maintenance required by modern day systems. Systems can be written in such a way that customers can prescribe their own remedies or vitamin supplements by simply changing data in tables.

The construction and manufacturing metaphors also create a separation between development and maintenance. Developers build things and maintainers fix them when they break. This separation has caused "we–they" problems that lie at the root of our personnel problems. Under these older metaphors, developers were treated like royalty and maintainers with disdain. If the metaphor is changed, the way we perceive software development and maintenance is changed forever.

What is needed is a new paradigm of software development and maintenance that models the laws of nature: software evolution. The evolutionary metaphor encourages us to think of IS and customers as parents that see their children through from conception to maturity. There is no separation, only a growing and expanding relationship between customer and IS, parent and system.

The evolutionary paradigm uses the metaphors of biological creation, growth, and evolution. Darwin thought of it over 100 years ago. Become aware of the possibilities as you discover how we can model successful growth and evolution of companies and their systems after nature's laws.

> *The evolution pattern of a large program is similar to that of any other complex system in that it stems from the closed-loop cyclic adaptation of the environment to system changes and vice versa.*
>
> *— L. A. Belady & M. M. Lehman*

Why do we need a new paradigm of software growth? To begin with, the development of most systems is based on *incomplete knowledge*. Like a baby born into the world, we don't have the knowledge to know what the system will become any more than we know what a baby will become. Any successful paradigm of software development must provide for learning and growth.

On a different level customers want systems delivered in a tenth the time; they want control of the system; and they want the system to be extremely reliable and massively flexible to meet the changing needs of the marketplace. Most executives and software engineers alike feel that there must be a better way. There never seems to be enough time to build the system "right"; IS never arrives at the right solution to the customer's problems; and the choice of technological solutions is becoming complex to the point of absurdity. Vendors, understanding these needs, have seduced IS management into large investments in CASE tools and massive methodologies, but alas, nothing seems to bring about the revolutionary change they seek. A typical application, when delivered, is incomplete and obsolete. Customers remain angry and distant as IS searches for ways to document its worth to the corporation.

Variations between people account for the biggest differences in software productivity.
                                                                    —Barry Boehm

When projects do succeed, it is often in spite of the methods and tools that were touted as the magical cure to productivity and quality diseases. Current software projects succeed because of the heroic efforts of a dedicated team rather than the successful application of methods and tools. People have been the key to software success and where they have succeeded, evolution was the key to their success.

The evolutionary paradigm supports prototyping in ways that construction and manufacturing cannot. Evolutionary prototyping, for example, is like a pregnancy—from conception to birth. Prototyping projects have *birth*days, not *dead*lines. Systems are born that will grow and evolve as opposed to being old and near death when delivered. If we used construction metaphors for babies, we'd take newborns and put them up on the shelf while we went off and attempted to build an adult from scratch.

Using the evolutionary paradigm, however, we can delight in the newborn and help it learn and grow continuously. A useful side benefit of this approach is that as the child learns and grows, we learn and grow along with it. The evolutionary paradigm allows for and supports the incompleteness of our knowledge. It allows us to learn as we go and change the system to meet our needs more easily.

Like systems built under the construction or manufacturing metaphor, evolutionary prototypes have a structure, but it is a living, flexible structure that supports growth and evolution. Evolutionary systems have an infancy where they need a lot of care. Constructed systems, when delivered, are old and need geriatric care. Evolutionary systems, because they continue to grow, have a childhood where they expand mentally and physically, an adolescence where they mature, and an adulthood where they typically achieve their full potential. Then, after a long life, they retire as a new wave of younger systems enters the workplace.

The evolutionary metaphor gives systems a character. Their character, however, is essentially in the hands of the people who animate them—you and me.

PROGRAMMER PRODUCTIVITY

Programmer productivity has been dragging along with meager increases of five percent or less per year. No investor would put their savings in an institution that delivers such a low rate of return. This pathetic level of improvement is no longer good enough. To meet the competitive challenges of the information economy of the next century, productivity and quality of software development and maintenance must grow rapidly. Information will be the key to running businesses in the global village. Vast improvements must take place if we are to achieve excellence in software.

The construction and manufacturing metaphors have constrained software to this level of improvement. A balanced evolution of people, processes, and technology will dramatically improve productivity and quality. Relying on technical panaceas has failed and it will continue to fail until IS departments establish adequate processes coupled with appropriate technology, and train their personnel in using both.

> *The major factor in wider propagation of professional methods is education, an education which conveys a broad and deep understanding of theoretical principles as well as their practical application.*
>
> *— C. A. Hoare*

To begin our journey from chaos to programmer productivity and software quality we'll look at the key role that training plays in achieving excellence. We will also need to look at the strategies companies must choose if they plan to participate in the information revolution. It all begins with people.

People

Projects consist of teams of people. The success or failure of a project depends largely on the team's organization, size of the team, how the team is formed, and how the team works together to accomplish their mission. To optimize productivity, projects must be chunked down into parts that can be handled by two to three people.

To optimize the buy-in and performance of a given team, the team needs to choose an approach that matches their problem or opportunity. To succeed at software prototyping, we will need to *consider the objective, not the tools to get us there.*

> *There's always a problem. No matter how it looks at first, it's always a people problem.*
> — *Gerald M. Weinberg*

Managers and customers complain about the quality of their systems and the time it takes to build them, and in the next breath they leap to axe the training budget. Investing in only tools and techniques reduces the chance for effective use. People create software, not machines or tools. Human relations have a direct effect on productivity and quality.

Furthermore, users complain that technoids talk down to them. Technicians complain that users are unsophisticated and don't know what they want. At the heart of this problem is the failure to establish a relationship before embarking on a software journey. Software projects are a marriage, not a battleground. The 1990s will see a revolution in training people to work with people. We must first develop rapport and then move toward specifying customer requirements. Without a sense of trust and of working together, customers get discouraged and hasten to end the discussion before they've really communicated their needs. Without the relationship required for successful requirements development, technical personnel will feel at odds and quickly turn toward their cold but familiar hardware and software.

Once communication is established, developers and users can truly begin to specify the desired system. Successful software efforts begin by first choosing the right project and then by developing the right requirements. Any useful process of creation focuses first on doing the "right work" and then on doing the "work right." Effectiveness is an essential goal. How the work gets done is secondary. Developers often fail to hear the user's "real" needs and wants. Instead they filter the user's desires through the engineering filter of their minds and deliver something undesirable. Immediate and ongoing cooperation ensures success.

Once the relationship flourishes, developers and customers can move into the actual creation of the system. In this involvement, developers, like young lovers, have a tendency to say "yes" to everything the customer requests. They forget to say "and it will cost this much and take this long." It's not unusual for a project to grow by 30–50 percent from the original requirements. During the development process, customers have a tendency to nibble away at the developers for more and more functionality. Again the developers forget to say "and it will cost this much and take this much longer." IS designers need basic skills in negotiating to deliver requirements that are both valid and reasonable from both perspectives.

With a good relationship and valid requirements, developers can begin to employ the methods and tools necessary to create the desired system. People are the knowledge repositories of the business.

Through specialization, large organizations can achieve increased productivity. One of the keys to software success is the use of education specialists to provide just-in-time training for all new methods and tools. Because of the shift in methodologies and technologies for software evolution, training will be required. This training breaks out into two key areas: general and specific training.

In an evolutionary model of the world, cells need to know the kinds of things that cells need to know. In the same way, software professionals need general training that can be environment independent or technology dependent. Operating systems, programming languages, data modeling, the relational data base model, and quality are all areas where general training is required and can be initiated immediately. General training in the methodology and technology cannot begin until they are selected and installed. Once all personnel receive the general training, certain key specialists will be needed.

In the evolutionary model again, cells of the liver need to know different things than brain cells. Specialized training for software professionals can also be environment independent or technology dependent. Standard activities like project management, change and configuration management, release management, and so on can begin immediately. Detailed training on specialized technology—both hardware and software—can begin when the development and production platforms are chosen.

Process and Tools

If effectiveness is the first goal of software development and maintenance, then the second goal is to create the user's desired system or modification as efficiently as possible. Efficiency focuses on using the right methods and tools to achieve the user's desires. Unfortunately for most software organizations, the effectiveness and efficiency of software development and maintenance remain pathetically low. To understand how low, we need to look at the current evolution and growth of IS departments toward maturity.

The Software Evolution metaphor suggests that software, companies, and markets don't build; they grow, change, and evolve. Business environments, as we know them, are not static and inflexible; they are dynamic, evolutionary, and at times, revolutionary. The construction paradigm is great if you want to set up camp in one place, but this often leads to inflexibility—hardening of the attitudes. In the seventieth anniversary issue of *Fortune* magazine, it identified that only 23 of the original Fortune 100 companies were still in business. Is it flexibility or rigidity that wins the day? Flexibility. Flexibility is the discipline of life, rigidity is the discipline of death.

To survive in the 1990s, companies must adopt a frame of mind that the status quo isn't good enough. To survive, we must all grow and continuously improve to meet the needs of changing markets, environments, and technology. Software Evolution is the paradigm of life and change.

The great oak tree does not spring forth, fully formed, from a tiny seed. Instead, nurtured from above by the sun and the rain, and nourished below by the earth, it grows and evolves to great size and strength.

—Lao Tzu

Software Evolution suggests that for software development to succeed, it must begin from the tiny seed of an idea or a concept and then grow, in stages, into adulthood. Just as we cannot give birth to a fully formed adult human being, we cannot gestate and give birth to a fully formed software system. There is too much to learn as a system grows.

EVOLUTION

The human brain has tripled in size in the last three million years. The hardware brain doubles in ability while halving in size every two years. The hardware evolution has produced many new generations of machines. Languages are classified as first, second, third, fourth, or fifth generation.

We use the terminology of evolution to define change in many areas of technology. Why not software?

In the thirteenth century, Saint Thomas Aquinas divided all created things into four classes (Bateson & Bateson 1987):

1. Those which just are, such as stones (or buildings)
2. Those which are and live, such as plants
3. Those which are and live and move, such as animals
4. Those which are and live and move and think—humans

Isn't it odd that with the construction or manufacturing metaphor that we are building software in the first class—things that are, inflexible things which are hard to maintain and change. Artificial intelligence and expert systems seem to be creating a fifth class—things which are and think. What would happen if we shifted the software metaphor to focus on things which are and live and move and think? Do growing things need diagrams to describe their architecture? Are growing things inflexible? Some growing things remain rooted in one place (i.e., plants) and others move effortlessly around (i.e., animals).

If we examine Darwin's theory of evolution, we see that he focused on evolution through "natural selection." That is, the best wins out and is passed on to the next generation. This is true of companies, the best quality at the best price is winning out in the marketplace. The best people can always find a job. Quality improvement evolves processes toward excellence. The best will always find a niche.

Evolution goes toward greater expansion and security of life. Evolution advances the organism from instinctive behavior to learned behavioral variety that can be passed from one being to another. Living beings go through four common stages of evolution:

1. Reacting to external stimuli—good or bad, safe or dangerous.
2. Reacting conditionally to external stimuli—fight or flight.
3. Increasing control of external stimuli using tools and techniques.
4. Communicating via symbols—words or pictures. Culture is a product of the human ability to communicate via symbols. Culture lives beyond the life span of any one individual.

Similarly, the companies with the best information systems will dominate the economy of the next decade and the next century. To have the best systems and the best information, companies must adopt an evolutionary strategy for their existing information systems. To cling to the old, inflexible strategy is the kiss of death. To embrace the future, we must abandon the stability we crave and develop a sense of mystery and curiosity about how to improve everything we do continuously. We must focus on achieving goals rather than on avoiding mistakes.

The love of continuous improvement is not first and foremost in the minds of most software developers and maintainers. This difficulty can most easily be noticed by observing the seeming obsession we have with new technology: CASE tools, object-oriented languages, and so on. We spend most of our lives hoping that the next technology will save us, or we'll win the lottery, or some other act of divine intervention will spirit us above the hectic, day-to-day activities of modern software work. This is a fool's errand.

We must shift from a culture that relies on the next miracle in technology to save us, to a culture that reveres the natural order of life. A culture that understands and enjoys the natural evolution of things will be surprised and delighted when some new innovation comes along to revolutionize some aspect of the work. As information industry workers, we must focus 80 percent of our attention on improving the day-to-day work and only 20 percent on the revolutions in methodology and technology that are occurring around us. If we don't know how to make small changes on a daily basis, how can we ever hope to be successful at making large revolutionary changes?

INNOVATION

As investigators discovered when researching Darwin's Theory of Evolution through Natural Selection, natural selection alone could not account for the full breadth of species on the planet. Other investigators observed that some deviation or mutation had to occur to create new species. In the software industry, such mutations are called by a better name—innovation.

Innovations are an essential part of creating new "life forms" for the information industry. It is evolution through natural selection that determines whether these new disciplines will survive. Structured programming survived. Data design survived. Object-oriented programming, the new kid on the block, is really the emergence of a technology that has been around since the 1960s. Business modeling, the next higher level of design life form, is vying for survival, and it most likely will, because higher level abstractions are necessary to define and re-engineer existing business processes adequately before they are automated.

The desktop computer has survived and is breeding at an extraordinary rate, only to be replaced every few years by a more powerful model with more features, more integration, and more flexibility in terms of connectivity and operability. Where once a terminal could only speak with one kind of computer, desktop workstations can communicate in any protocol with almost anyone. Where once the user interface consisted of 25 lines of 80 characters, there are now graphics and text and sound and animation capabilities integrated in one machine. Where once there were QWERTY keyboards, there are now mice and light pens and touch screens and voice recognition.

A combination of innovation and evolution have brought these tools to market. Engineering is a discipline of innovation and evolution. A new idea brings about the creation of a prototype and from there hundreds or thousands of tiny tinkerings and tailorings evolve the product into a finished product. The space program of the 1960s underwent many major evolutionary steps—Mercury, Gemini, Apollo—and many stepwise improvements in every rocket, capsule, and ground-based system. The Macintosh followed a similar course. The Xerography process has undergone continual improvement. Xerox, for example, has set a goal of reducing copier production costs by 50 percent and a fourfold improvement in reliability between 1989 and 1992. The majority of the effort occurs during evolution, not the original innovation. Why should software be any different?

It is impossible that man should not be part of nature, or that he should not follow her general order.

—Spinoza

The answer is that software isn't any different, we just want to believe it is so that we can feel a certain jolt of being better than the next guy or that we are involved in some important new mission for humanity. But can a blade of grass be better than a tree? Can one person be better than the next? Or is everything equally important in the scheme of things?

NATURE

For the moment, let's look at nature and her plan for living things. "Nature is the structure of evolving processes," suggests Alfred North Whitehead

(Miller 1978). Life is made up of systems of systems. Information systems are extensions of our natural abilities.

The essential element of life is the cell. *All* life forms begin as a single cell. It came as a surprise to me to discover that we retrace our evolutionary history in the womb. Beginning as a single cell, we grow into a fetus with *gill slits* which are later transformed as we develop lungs. Still later we grow a complete covering of hair and a tail and then shed the hair and reabsorb the tail. The single original cell multiplies and at particular points the cells differentiate into specific organs and limbs and nervous tissue.

Plants begin from a single cell cocooned in a seed of nourishment which may lie dormant for dozens or hundreds of years before finding the proper conditions to grow. As the cells divide, some become roots and push down into the soil and others rise up above the soil into the sun, becoming stems and leaves and flowers through differentiation.

Single-celled plants and animals still abound in oceans, rivers, and lakes. Some can make us ill and others feed the giant blue whale.

Cells rely on heredity to determine how to grow and reproduce. Chromosomes carry the genes that are merely combinations of certain kinds of atoms, which, at the lowest level, consist of protons, neutrons, and electrons and sundry other particles. In a sense, everything relies on the underlying structure that came before it—particles, atoms, genes, chromosomes, cells, organs, organisms, family units, and entire cultures.

In the book *Living Systems* (Miller 1978), the author describes the structure and process of the seven hierarchical levels of living systems: cell, organ, organism, group, organization, society, and supranational system. Each of these systems are "open systems composed of other subsystems which process inputs, throughputs, and outputs of various forms of matter, energy, and information." Sounds vaguely like the general theory of information systems, doesn't it?

Miller continues by identifying 19 critical subsystems which process energy, matter, and information (Table 1.1) which are essential to successful continuation of the overall system. Not surprisingly, these subsystems are the same as one would expect to see in any information program or system. Any system mutation that inhibits any one of these critical subsystems will cause the overall system to be eliminated by natural selection. Study the systems that have expired or been replaced by other systems in your organization; which subsystem took it off the evolutionary path?

The natural direction of evolution is toward more complex systems, and yet they are all based on simple evolutionary stepping stones, cells. The information economy has seen the same evolution—the complex systems of the 1960s are child's play compared to the systems of the 1990s, which

TABLE 1.1   19 Critical Subsystems

Subsystem	Action or Process
Information and Matter-Energy Processors	
Reproducer	Creates similar subsystems
Boundary	Perimeter that holds components together, protects them from environmental stresses, excludes or permits entry to various sorts of matter-energy and information
Matter-Energy Processors	
Ingestor	Brings matter-energy across the boundary from the environment into the system
Distributor	Carries inputs from outside the system or outputs from its subsystems to each of its components
Converter	Changes inputs into more useful forms for special processes
Producer	Balances associations among inputs and outputs
Matter-energy storage	Retains deposits of various sorts of matter-energy
Extruder	Transmits matter-energy out of the system in the forms of products or wastes
Motor	Moves the system or parts in relation to the environment
Supporter	Maintains spatial relationships among components of the system so that they can interact without weighting each other down or crowding each other
Information Processors	
Input transducer	Brings information into the system and transforms it as required
Internal transducer	Transforms and transmits information within the system
Channel and net	Transmission network among nodes of the network
Decoder	Changes the public information given it into private code for internal consumption
Associator	First stage of the learning process—forms enduring associations among items of information in the system
Memory	Second stage of learning—stores information in the system for different periods of time
Decider	Executive that receives and transmits information that controls the whole system
Encoder	Changes private, internal information into public information that can be shared by other systems in the environment
Output transducer	Transforms and transmits information into the system's environment

Source: Adapted with permission. Miller, *Living Systems,* 1978, McGraw-Hill, p. 3.

will seem simple when compared to the information systems of the next century. As evolution continues, each of the seven levels of the hierarchy becomes more complex and also more effective. Specialization has its advantages.

SOFTWARE

As we penetrate into matter, nature does not show us any isolated "basic building blocks," but rather appears as a complicated web of relations between various parts of the whole.
— *Fritjof Capra—The Tao of Physics*

If we begin now to think about software along the same lines as nature, we can begin to see and feel how they are similar. Hardware is like the body; software is the mind; and data the food that nourishes the whole system.

All software and data are formed from two things: 0 and 1 (Figure 1.1). Binary is the atomic unit of all software. From this, we can compose characters and data elements and data structures and databases. From binary, we can also compose the instructions of the consciousness (code) that will direct the body (computer) to consume, digest, process, and reshape the data in such a way that humans can consume it more effectively or it can trigger other machines to perform their tasks.

Thus we begin to see that hardware, software, and data are one component in a larger system that includes people and their processes and the other machines they employ. Software Evolution is concerned with not just the microcosm of the computer, but the larger system of people, business, and the world as well. How can a patient be healed if only his or her symptoms are treated and not the underlying root cause of the illness? How can a business be healed if we treat the symptoms of declining revenues with amputation of expenses like employees and training and all of the things that create growth in a company? The wellness of our businesses, our lives, and our world is becoming more dependent in many ways on the health of our software. The rigidity and inflexibility of our existing systems should be cause for alarm.

If we don't change how we are creating information systems, we will be hopelessly mired in our own morass of inflexibility. All of mankind could become maintenance programmers for the very machines we invented to save us time and energy. Anyone who has worked in the industry for very long knows how challenging and stressful it can be to build or maintain "good" software. Anyone who has been around long enough has seen that

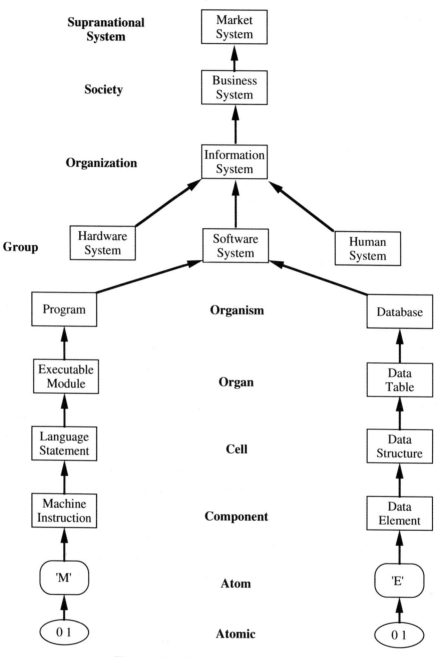

Figure 1.1   Software evolutionary tree

successful systems grow from small seeds that are continuously cared for and nurtured and evolved to ensure their success. The ones that are the most painful started small, but were allowed to grow uncontrolled for years without weeding, pesticides, or trimming. And now the jungle is dense and overgrown and filled with poisonous spiders and snakes and programmer-eating plants and animals that consume young men and women through exorbitant overtime and endless nights in the computer center and then spit them out like a parrot might spit out empty seeds.

What we need is a way to evolve continuously both our people, processes, technology, and products to meet existing needs. Fortunately, such a way already exists. In fact, any place that people are succeeding at any task, the evolutionary process can be found at work. I call it the life cycle of life cycles.

THE LIFE CYCLE OF LIFE CYCLES

Although it has been around for perhaps as long as humans have walked the earth, the life cycle of life cycles was first documented by Dr. Shewhart at Bell Labs in 1938. The Shewhart cycle (Figure 1.2), or PDCA, is the cornerstone of all evolutionary processes, including continuous quality improvement.

For example, let's look at the waterfall life cycle (Royce 1970) for software development (Figure 1.3). Requirements and design are both planning processes. Coding is the actual ''doing'' of the system. And testing checks the system, following which, the developers act to improve the requirements, design, and code. Unfortunately, the delay between plan and check was so long that major problems were often overlooked until it was too late to re-engineer the system.

Royce, the originator of the waterfall model, said it had been simplified and misinterpreted. The original model supported the engineering processes of prototyping and increment refinements to arrive at the final product. Successful development, he said, should rely on these two techniques to build the right system right the first time.

Another software crisis stems from maintaining existing software. ''We'll fix it in the maintenance phase,'' management says, and, of course, it isn't true because they would always be too busy trying to keep the system up to date, so the system would slowly slide into decay and need to be replaced. This process is tremendously wasteful and yet corporations turn to it repeatedly to replace the previous system that didn't live up to expectations.

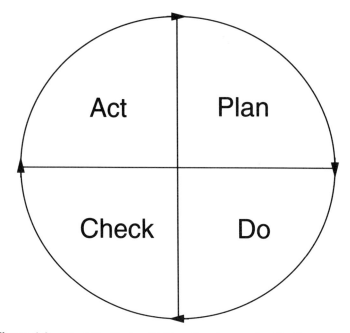

Figure 1.2   The Life Cycle of Life—Continuous Quality Improvement

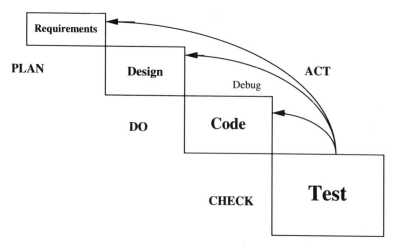

Figure 1.3   Waterfall Life Cycle

To circumvent these long delays, the inspection or walkthrough process is used to check each interim system product before sending it on to the next step (Figure 1.4). Once the developer works with the customer to *plan* the system, the developer can write the requirements (*do*) and then schedule a walkthrough or inspection (*check*). Based on the results of the inspection, the developer can then *act* to improve the requirements. Typically, only one or two rounds of revisions are made before someone starts getting anxious and the process moves into the next step in the waterfall. The same process usually occurs in design and code, but few revisions are allowed per design or program. And sometimes, by this point the project is so far behind schedule that no inspections are held and the project heads for extinction.

At this point, software professionals miss another opportunity. The results of inspections are typically used to improve the product—requirements, design, code, or data. Unfortunately, this means that you never get to the root cause of schedule slippages and cost overruns; you never get to the root cause of missed requirements, poor design, and unmaintainable code; you never get better. To evolve as a company and as a person, you must use the PDCA cycle to improve the process you use to create requirements, designs, code, data, documentation, or training. Otherwise, you'll never become excellent at software.

Every check or test is an important point to collect data about what's working and what isn't. Unfortunately, most companies never notice the

Requirements

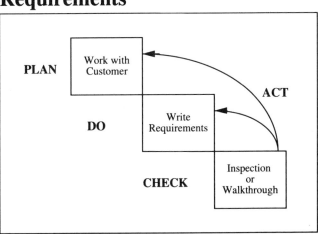

Figure 1.4 Inspections

Requirements

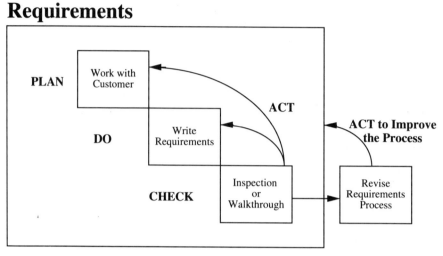

Figure 1.5   Requirements Process

opportunity missed and go right on doing things the way they have always done them, racing headlong toward extinction. Using the information from each walkthrough, inspection, or test, you can begin to analyze the data to identify the root causes of problems in the software process and begin doing something to correct them. In the requirements example shown in Figure 1.5, developers could analyze the common problems that repeatedly occur in the requirements process and then act to improve the requirements process. This is the essence of continuous quality improvement.

The 1990s is the decade of quality improvement. If you apply PDCA to improve your processes as well as your products, you will survive and grow. If you don't use quality improvement, you will most likely become extinct. The future belongs to those who can create tactical and strategic application systems that are ''good, fast, and cheap.'' Only through quality improvement can you achieve all three of these criteria.

RAPID PROTOTYPING AND SOFTWARE CREATION

How does PDCA apply to rapid prototyping and software creation? If we look at the waterfall model, there is such a long lead time between requirements and the user's acceptance of the system that there is still plenty of time for problems to slip by and foul the deliverable system beyond repair.

PDCA = Plan Do Check Act

Specified requirements have to be read and understood and then the customer has to make a mental picture of how the system will work. It's like the difference between describing how to hit a baseball and showing someone how to hit one using a bat and a ball. Behavioral demonstrations always carry the most information and are least prone to improper interpretation. This suggests that there is a high risk associated with ''construction'' projects even though inspections and walkthroughs are cleaning up some of the problems before they are built into the system.

The way to begin reducing the risk is to shorten the time between the customer's expression of a need and the developer's demonstration of the capability. The only way this can be accomplished is through rapid application of the PDCA process to first gather the customer's requirements, create a prototype, and test it by working with the customer to compare it against their existing and as yet unknown requirements. Often, until you can demonstrate something to a customer, he or she won't be able to clearly articulate what they need.

Another way to reduce the risk is to allow for more than two revisions of the prototype. Prototyping relies on dozens, hundreds, or even thousands of corrections and improvements. An airplane, en route to its destination, is off course over 90 percent of the time. Airplanes arrive at their destinations, however, by continuously adjusting their course *in flight*. Very often, when a project takes off, customers don't exactly know where they want to go. Only through continuous adjustment can the system and customers arrive at the desired destination. Compare this to the ''construction'' model that encouraged us to believe that we could specify where we wanted to go before we left the ground and then rarely shift course as we rushed to meet the deadline. Rather than head toward a destination, we flew until we ran out of gas or time and then set the project down wherever we happened to be. Then we'd ask the passengers (customers) whether this was where they wanted to be. Most of the time it wasn't, so we put them on a variety of maintenance and enhancement flights which took short hops in the direction they wanted to go.

Another way to reduce risk is to limit the prototyping process to just the customer's needs, excluding their wants and wishes. The waterfall model led us to attempt to specify all of the customer's requirements. These efforts were often off by 50 percent or more. With rapid prototyping, the prototyper focuses on only creating the 20 percent of the system that will provide 80 percent of the value. The rest of the system will be added by growth and evolution. This helps the prototyping team arrive at the customer's desired destination more quickly than was ever conceived possible.

Notice that evolutionary prototypes are never disposable. Like a baby, an evolutionary prototype is created with the intention of delivering it. Like pregnancy, the prototyping process can be stopped easily in the first third of the creation process if the fetal system is genetically defective or it appears that it may endanger the parents. In the second third of creating a prototype, the project can still be stopped, but it requires understanding and effort. In the final third, you are better off to deliver the prototype than to stop it. Any structural and genetic changes can be done after delivery.

In the construction paradigm, I've seen huge systems devour resources that could easily have killed the parent company. Managers and programmers become so obsessed with continuing the development that they fail to take into consideration the cost of the system. Unlike the old beliefs about prototyping, a prototype is not something to refine the requirements before we get on with the real work of the development project. Evolutionary prototyping, like pregnancy, creates the first working version of the system. The "baby" is then *delivered* into the real world and its customer and IS parents help it grow into the powerful and helpful offspring it was meant to be.

SOFTWARE MATURITY FRAMEWORK

Software is a place where dreams are planted and nightmares harvested, where terrible demons compete with magical panaceas, a world of werewolves and silver bullets.

— Brad Cox

The Software Engineering Institute (SEI) at Carnegie Mellon has a series of software initiatives under investigation for the Department of Defense. One of these initiatives involves software processes and their evolution from infancy to adulthood. The Software Maturity Framework (Humphrey 1988 and 1989) describes the five levels of software process maturity that were observed by SEI's process improvement team. I call it the stairway to software excellence (Figure 1.6).

There are five steps on the stairway to software excellence: chaos, project management, methods and tools, measurement, and continuous quality improvement. These five steps represent the actual evolutionary path of successful software organizations. To be successful at rapid evolutionary development, an IS organization must reach at least the third level, where the methods and tools required are defined, installed, and used. Three elements inhibit movement toward software excellence:

1. Crisis and fire fighting
2. Process change, which consumes resources for retraining and use
3. Cultural change

Based on assessments conducted with hundreds of companies, the SEI concluded that the vast majority of U.S. software companies are still stuck in the initial or second phase of software maturity. Crisis and fire fighting trap these companies in archaic methods and tools. Few companies have risen from the tar pit described by Brooks (1975). Those that have pulled themselves out of the tar are living in a harsh world where software processes are barely defined, tools are poorly chosen and ill trained, and personnel follow technology like nomadic tribes follow wild game. Like the generations before us, there is only one way to rise above our almost imperceptible evolution: IS organizations must invest equally in people, processes, and tools to achieve productive, high-quality software creation and evolution.

It takes 18–24 months to traverse each step of the stairway to software excellence because of the training and cultural transformation required. A balanced approach that integrates people with the software processes and tools required will succeed. The journey begins with an assessment of your location on the stairway to software excellence. The full SEI assessment can be obtained by U.S. companies from the National Technologi-

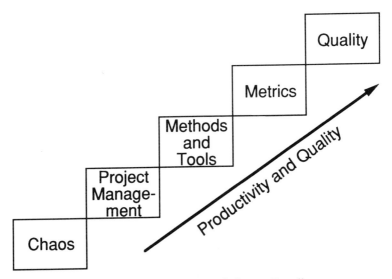

Figure 1.6 The Stairway to Software Excellence

cal, Information Service (NTIS) (Humphrey & Kitson 1987). The assessment will help you determine where you are on the road from chaos to quality.

Chaos

The first step of the stairway, chaos, is the tar pit Brooks (1975) described. The tar pit turned out to be an apt analogy because so many extinct species of animals can now be found in the La Brea tar pits, and those IS organizations that remain in chaos will ultimately drag themselves and their company down into the software tar pit. Chaos causes cost overruns and project failures and customer anger and alienation. At this point, managers and programmers don't trust each other; fire fighting reigns supreme; and there is no time to think about how to do things better. It seems that IS keeps slipping back into the tar pit. Software creation and evolution demands that IS begin pulling itself up out of the tar pit and slowly, one stair at a time, begin moving up the stairway to software excellence.

And how do you discover where you are on the stairway to software excellence? By applying the check part of the PDCA process: most likely you've already been planning and doing software development and maintenance; now you can begin your journey to software excellence by taking the simple self assessment in Figure 1.7. By answering this simple yes or no questionnaire to the best of your understanding, you'll get a feeling of where you are on the stairway to software excellence. I encourage you to do this now before you read any farther, because the results may surprise you.

Any sufficiently advanced technology is indistinguishable from magic.
— *Arthur C. Clarke*

This assessment doesn't mean that organizations that are still in chaos cannot begin trying to use rapid evolutionary development; it's just that they may not be as successful. If in the search for microwave solutions you stumble on rapid evolutionary development, don't blame the process if you fail to put the foundations in place to ensure its success.

The "SEI reported that 74 percent of surveyed organizations were at what it calls the 'Initial' phase of evolution" (Moad 1990). To effectively use rapid evolutionary development, IS must achieve at least the critical elements of the second step of the stairway: project management.

Repeatable

Yes/No

Y N   Do you have a software quality assurance (SQA) function?

Y N   Do you use software configuration control?

Y N   Do you formally review each software project's contribution prior to making commitments?

Y N   Do you formally estimate software size, effort, and cost?

Y N   Do you formally plan software schedules?

Y N   Do you measure and track the size and complexity of each software module over time?

Y N   Do you measure and track errors/defects throughout the maintenance life cycle?

Y N   Does management formally review the status of software projects?

Y N   Do you use a mechanism to control changes to the software requirements?

<u>Y N</u>   Do you use a mechanism to control who changes the code and when?

        If the number of yes answers exceeds seven, give yourself **REPEATABLE**.

Defined

Y N   Do you use a standardized and documented software maintenance process on each project?

Y N   Is there a software engineering process group that evolves the maintenance process?

Y N   Is there a required software engineering training program for software professionals?

Y N   Do you measure and track software design errors and defects?

Y N   Do you conduct internal software design reviews/inspections?

Y N   Are the action items resulting from design reviews tracked to closure?

Y N   Do you use a mechanism to control changes to the software design?

Y N   Do you conduct software code reviews/inspections?

Y N   Are the action items resulting from code reviews tracked to closure?

Y N   Is there a formal training program for design and code review leaders?

Y N   Do you use a mechanism used to ensure compliance with the software engineering standards?

<u>Y N</u>   Do you formally verify the adequacy of regression testing?

        If the number of yes answers exceeds nine, give yourself **DEFINED**.

(continued)

Figure 1.7   Software Evolution: Quick Assessment

Managed

Y N   Is a formal mechanism used to manage the introduction of new technologies?
Y N   Are requirements, design, and code review standards applied?
Y N   Are design, code, and test errors estimated and compared to actuals?
Y N   Are design and code review coverages measured and recorded?
Y N   Is the design review data analyzed to evaluate the product and reduce future defects?
Y N   Is test coverage measured and recorded for each phase of functional testing?
Y N   Has a metrics database been established for process measurement across all projects?
Y N   Is the error data from code reviews and tests analyzed to determine the likely distribution and characteristics of the errors remaining in the product?
Y N   Are analyses of errors conducted to determine their process-related causes?
Y N   Is review efficiency analyzed for each project?
<u>Y N</u>   Is a mechanism used for periodically assessing the software engineering process and implementing indicated improvements?
       If the number of yes answers exceeds eight, give yourself **MANAGED**.

Optimized

Y N   Is a mechanism used for identifying and replacing obsolete technologies?
Y N   Is a mechanism used for error cause analysis?
Y N   Are the error causes reviewed to determine the process changes required to prevent them?
<u>Y N</u>   Is a mechanism used for initiating error prevention actions?
       If the number of yes answers exceeds two, give yourself **OPTIMIZED**.

Tools and Technology

Do the software development and maintenance personnel use:
Y N   Automated configuration control to manage software changes throughout the process?
Y N   A high-order language?
Y N   Interactive source-level debuggers?
Y N   Interactive documentation facilities?
<u>Y N</u>   Computer tools for tracking and reporting the status of the software in the library?
       If the number of yes answers exceeds three, give yourself **AUTOMATED**.

Figure 1.7   *(continued)*

Project Management

In the SEI model, this step is known as the *Repeatable* step and it is characterized by the use of project management and control of costs, schedules, commitments, and changes. To achieve this step, an IS organization must have a way to manage change to evolving systems (change management), a way to manage the various configurations of system components and parts (configuration management), and a systematic way to schedule the work requested by the customer (project management). IS organizations can begin by:

- **Plan**

  Formally planning software releases and schedules

- **Do**

  Formally estimating software size, effort, and cost

  Using a process to manage changes to the requirements, design, code, documentation, and training (change management)

  Using a process to control versions and changes to system parts and components (software configuration management)

- **Check**

  Formally reviewing each project's contribution to the business (Do we need this new baby? Are we doing the right work?). Using quality terminology, policy deployment integrates and focuses all work on key business strategies

  Formally reviewing the status of software projects

  Measuring and tracking errors or defects and the size and complexity of each software module over time

  Implementing a Software Quality Assurance (SQA) function to monitor the improvements in products and processes using the measurement data

The second level of process maturity offers the shelter of some basic, repeatable processes for succeeding at software development. Project management, change control, configuration management, and initial quality assurance begin to take form. This level relies on software heroes who have lived through enough projects to know the tar pits and how to avoid them. Unfortunately, these people have the power and managers tend to deify them because of their "innate abilities." To rise to the next level, someone else typically models the hero's behavior in enough detail that they can write it down and share it with others.

Methods and Tools

Poor methodology lies at the root of modern software problems.
— *Harlan Mills*

Once the basic processes are in place, IS organizations can climb to the next step by beginning to define and automate the software development process. In the SEI model, this step is called *Defined*, meaning that before IS can evolve any farther, it must define the process used for both software creation and evolution. The rapid evolutionary development process is significantly different from the construction process and the evolution process is different from the maintenance process. This book describes the rapid evolutionary development process in detail and Arthur (1988) describes the evolution process in detail. With these processes as a baseline, an IS organization can then choose the tools needed to support the process. Most IS organizations go awry by picking their tools before they know *what* they intend to do and *how* they intend to do it. This is similar to going to the hardware store and buying a tool before you knew what you needed. The tool kit for rapid evolutionary development will be significantly different from the tool kit used to build systems from scratch.

The first priority of a software process is to *prevent* defects rather than detect and remove them. Human verification can replace debugging (Mills, Dyer, & Linser 1987). "Even informal human verification can produce software sufficiently robust to go to system test without debugging. Human verification need take *no more time* than debugging." More than 90 percent of total product defects were found before first execution, which is significantly higher than normal. Human verification also results in a drop in total defects.

Other organizations go awry by forcing their people to use the tool even though it doesn't fit the process they are using: "Here's a hammer; go screw in that light bulb." This alienates the prototyper and the customer, and it delivers pathetic results.

To move from the second step, repeatable, to a defined process, you will need:

- A process group to continuously evolve the software processes
- Processes for creation and evolution
- Technology to support both processes

The third level of process maturity uses a defined process (i.e., written) that can be used by everyone. The heroes of the *repeatable* stage struggle as they attempt to retain their power, but find it gone. A new hero arises that can hold the defined process up to the people like a tablet of commandments. The process can be 12 pages long, as DeMarco might suggest in his seminar, or it can be hundreds of pages long and completely unintelligible. If you think about pregnancy, there is no defined process. Instead, the process is organic and instinctive. Software processes are not at the level of instinctive, so some guidance is necessary. I lean toward DeMarco's suggestion of a few pages that describe the PDCA cycle for the project.

The processes for creation and evolution must be simple enough to be taught easily. Training must elevate skills to the level that IS personnel can create the software demanded by their customers. A group must be empowered to maintain and improve the software process and training.

There are perhaps three main processes used in the software industry: structured programming that focuses on the processing of data, information engineering that focuses on the data first, and real-time programming that focuses on events. Data-focused design and programming are the best way to design evolutionary business systems. We can then use structured design and programming to create the procedural components. Object-oriented programming is just another form of data-focused software creation. Real-time designers and programmers focus on the abilities of the system to handle simple and then increasingly more complex events.

If you think about the human body, it is a system—an organism. From an object-oriented point of view, the body is composed of many organs, each of which have their own special function. Each organ consists of many cells that have structure and processing. It's not that rapid evolutionary development throws away all of the things that you know about software. Instead, it reorganizes them to make them more useful.

To move to the defined level of software process maturity, everyone, including managers, must be trained in the process or methodology chosen. This can be a very costly step, especially if you choose a methodology that doesn't fit your organization. It can also be costly if you try to retrofit a process to the ragtag collection of software technology and tools that you've accumulated over a decade.

To automate the defined step, you must first choose a process that matches the way people work. Again, the evolutionary paradigm fits the way we are and the way we live. Then, and only then, should you choose an integrated suite of tools to match the process chosen. It's also useful to have a flexible methodology and technology kit that can be used interchangeably to configure processes and tools to the project at hand. Small projects, for example, don't need as much rigor as large ones do. Match the methods and tools to the scope of the project.

Achieving this third level of process maturity requires the largest investment that any company will typically ever make. There must be resources spent to identify and purchase matching methodologies and technologies, and more money spent to train the personnel that are going to use it. Let's face it, we wouldn't put a pilot into an airline cockpit without training. We wouldn't expect surgeons to do surgery without an education, but we expect untrained programmers, analysts, and managers to create software using hastily purchased methods and tools. Then we wonder why they can't perform! IS departments spend a tremendous amount of money and time creating a software cockpit and then fail to train the people that will fly and maintain it. Then we wonder what went wrong and blame the process for being too old or the tool for being too complex, when oftentimes we've simply failed to train the other vital component in the system—the human that operates them. Peters and other top consultants tell us that to achieve competitive advantage, we must train, train, train, and yet few of us listen.

There is a price you have to pay to be excellent at anything, whether it's a sport or a hobby or software. If you want to be the best, you have to learn how to be excellent. Training and education precede the achievement of excellence. Trying to train people after they've learned how to ''get by'' is often a challenge. First, we have to help them unlearn what they know and then lead them to the ''right'' way. One of the ways to help determine the right way is to get hard facts about what works and what doesn't through measurement.

Measurement

The mere act of measuring human processes changes them.
— *Watts S. Humphrey*

Software measurement is actually a refined science that can greatly assist any organization in becoming excellent. The only problem is that most IS organizations aren't mature enough to use metrics wisely to improve the process—they use them to measure people and to compare one group to another, which creates turf and resentment, and crushes morale, productivity, and quality. To succeed at software measurement, it must be used to assess current quality problems and then as a foundation for improvement of both effectiveness and efficiency.

Software measurement of defects and evolutionary enhancements can help an organization pinpoint the hot spots in a given system so that they can be genetically re-engineered or rewritten to eliminate effort. Software measurement can help programmers know when they've exceeded the natural limits of a program or module's size and complexity and they should begin looking for another way to redesign the product to improve its flexibility and evolutionary capability. In nature, cells do not grow to the size of a kidney; they divide and multiply to form a kidney. Cells have a built-in measurement device that tells them when it's time to divide and form more cells. Programmers typically have no such internal instrumentation. There are simply no excuses for modules larger than 300 noncommentary source lines, as we will see in Chapter 2, Natural Laws.

"Once the discipline of statistical quality control is in place, management can see the development process and can control process changes to control product quality" (Mills 1987). Incremental development of software, using rapid evolutionary development, permits realistic measurements of quality.

Much of the measurement data available today goes to waste because no one bothers to look at it and when they do they don't have the knowledge to use it wisely. This is not unexpected, however, since most companies are barely out of the tar pit. The companies really don't care for people who walk up with a yardstick and a stop watch and say things like, "It took you almost 30 years to climb out of that swamp, but I want you to run the 100 yard dash in under 10 seconds."

It takes a certain amount of trust to collect measurements that will be of any value. Otherwise, people will falsify the data or create wild scenarios to justify their results. They have to know what the measurements will be used for and how they are being used.

To establish a managed process, you will need:

- Process measurements based on the defined software processes
- A measurement database for historical tracking
- A way to assess results and recommend improvements

The fourth step toward software excellence, *managed*, begins to implement the quality improvement process through measurement. Where measurements were once used as a tool to flog unsuspecting programmers, measurement will become the cornerstone for identifying problems in software processes or tools. Measurements will show management where to make the improvements necessary to maximize productivity and quality. It's almost impossible to move to the fifth and final level without a measurement program in place. Function point metrics, lines of code, and complexity measurements will join with other measures of time and resources to expand our understanding of the development and maintenance process. Software process measurement will allow IS to move to the highest level of software process maturity—continous quality improvement.

Continuous Quality Improvement

The 1980s saw America go from a creditor nation to a debtor nation, from a budget surplus to a budget deficit, from a world leader to a camp follower. The Japanese, with the help of W. Edwards Deming, have created an epidemic of quality that has moved out of manufacturing into fields of finance (Japanese banks hold seven out of the top ten positions) and they are moving into software in a big way.

The 1990s will be the time for America to turn to continuous quality improvement, or slide into decay. Since the world is already a largely information-based economy, software will spell the winners and losers of the next decade and perhaps the next century. Anyone who fails to discover PDCA and use it to their advantage will most likely go the way of the dinosaurs.

Measurements provide the data to fuel the improvement process. By analyzing the data, software people can identify where and how to improve software processes. Improving processes maximizes productivity, quality, and customer satisfaction, while reducing costs and price. This spells competitive advantage and competitive advantage spells success.

Continuous quality improvement helps managers understand where to spend resources effectively to improve the process and therefore the products produced. It lets prototypers communicate with facts not just gut feel, and it provides prototypers with the skills to optimize their work.

Plan Do Check Act

Strangely enough, if you look at the stairway to software excellence or the SEI maturity framework, you'll notice that the second step—repeatable project management—focuses on better *planning*. The third step—defined creation and evolution processes—focuses on *doing* a better job of software development through specified methods and matching tools. The fourth step—managing software through measurement—focuses on instrumenting the processes using metrics to *check* how everything is working. And the final step—optimizing the process through continuous quality improvement—focuses on taking *action* to improve the people, processes, and tools to maximize results and minimize costs.

It does not matter how slowly you go, as long as you do not stop.

— Confucius

The stairway is nothing more than a much larger version of the PDCA process. The good news, as Peters says, is that you can start today, the bad news is that you're never finished. Advancing up each step of the stairway can take 18–24 months. Continuous evolution and improvement of all aspects of people, processes, and tools are required to keep the competitive edge created through this organizational growth.

SUMMARY

In this chapter, you've been introduced to a new way of looking at software development that shifts your perceptual filters from the old construction paradigm to the evolution paradigm. You may have discovered that these older metaphors of construction, manufacturing, and the waterfall model trap us in ways of creating software that are inefficient and ineffective. By changing the metaphors we live by, we can change the results we receive from the software we create.

You've also learned how a timeless life cycle of life cycles, PDCA, guides everything we do with software creation and evolution. Using the SEI model, PDCA even guides the growth and evolution of software excellence in companies like yours.

Now that you understand the basics of Software Evolution, it's time to look at the natural laws that give Software Evolution and Rapid Evolutionary Development their tremendous power and simplicity.

CHAPTER 2

The Natural Laws of Software Evolution

The intellectual life may be kept clean and healthful if man will live the life of nature and not import into his mind difficulties which are none of his.
—Ralph Waldo Emerson

Natural law implies a universal order of things. The evolutionary perspective transforms the physical balance of natural law into a continually expanding and growing order of change. Sometimes it takes a lot of experience to see nature's laws clearly and once seen clearly, natural laws can almost always be stated simply.

Let us draw a lesson from nature, which always works by short ways.
—Ralph Waldo Emerson

The first, and perhaps the most obvious, law is:

If it's simple, it must be part of the solution;
If it's complex, it must be part of the problem.

We've all heard the KISS (keep it simple stupid) principle, but then we immediately turn around and make everything complex. Is it the need for job security or just the delusion that technology has to be complex?

It is a simple task to make things complex, it is a complex task to make things simple.

—*Tom DeMarco (1989)*

The problem is not stupidity, but an ignorance of the natural laws of software that contort our information systems. Why are we ignorant of the natural laws of software engineering? Lack of understanding and education. If you think education is expensive, try ignorance.

A BRIEF LESSON IN HISTORY

Natural laws in software engineering are not new. To my knowledge the earliest mention is in an article by Belady and Lehman (1976). In the article, they stated that their "first observations encouraged the search for models that represented laws that governed the dynamic behavior of the *metasystem* of organization, people, and program material involved in the creation and maintenance process, in the evolution of programming systems." In other words, information systems are part of a *metasystem* that includes people and organizations. To help us understand these models, we can begin to look at the natural laws that make them work. The authors then went on to identify "laws of program evolution." These three laws are worth reviewing:

- **Law of Continuing Change**

  A system that is used will undergo continuing change until it is judged more cost effective to freeze and recreate it.

  This law suggests that as the business environment changes, so must the software. This law also suggests that we can take an organic system and put it into suspended animation (freeze it) while we bring up a new generation to replace it.

- **Law of Increasing Entropy**

  The entropy of a system (its unstructuredness) increases with time, unless specific work is executed to maintain or reduce it.

  Entropy comes from a Greek word meaning transformation. Oddly enough, software systems rarely develop entropy unless changes are made to them that do not take into account the overall ecology of the metasystem. It seems that if we can transform software into antiquated junk, we could also transform it, via evolutionary re-engineering, into newness and excellence.

Software that does not change to meet the changing needs of the business, however, is developing entropy. James Miller says that "Entropy always increases in a walled off system. To go uphill against entropy, systems must be open to new inputs that restore their own energy and repair breakdowns in their organized structure" (1979). In essence, software needs to be flexible enough to handle all kinds of new data that extend the software's abilities and also resilient to defects.

• **Law of Statistically Smooth Growth**

Growth trend measures of global system attributes may appear to be stochastic locally in time and space, but statistically, they are cyclically self-regulating, with well-defined long-range trends. The system and the metasystem—the project organization that is developing it—constitute an organism that is constrained by conservation laws. The system and the metasystem are interacting systems.

By this Belady and Lehman (1976) mean that the software system and organization that support and use it grow in steady cycles over a period of time. Notice that this law implies the organic nature of software development. They even go on to state that "the 'laws' that we are expounding upon have gradually evolved. . . ." Evolution seems to crop up everywhere. Now let's look at some other natural laws of software evolution.

General Laws

No one can get it right the first time. There will always be some way to do it better the next time. Using PDCA, we can identify those better ways.

Development is full of surprises. Software development is based on *insufficient knowledge.* Therefore, we can and should expect some delightful surprises as we learn about the developing system.

Corollary: *The typical development project floats in a sea of changes.*

No matter how good the system is, users will make mistakes using it. People and, therefore, users are different. They can and will do things that you anticipate.

The Law of the Fossil Record

Living systems leave records of their existence. We often hear developers speak in terms of system *artifacts*. Software systems also leave records:

1. *The most primitive forms of life are found in the oldest rocks.* (If you don't believe me, check any system over 25 years old. It's probably written in assembly language.)
2. *Moving up through the various strata, there is a succession of higher and more complex forms of life.* In software, there has been a steady evolution of languages—Assembly, Fortran, COBOL, and so on. User interfaces have grown from punch cards, to line-by-line terminals, to graphical interfaces. Hardware has gone through many generations of evolution.
3. *A life form may lie dormant for many years before it becomes dominant through adaptive radiation* (e.g., UNIX).
4. *There have been many large extinctions, but some species have always survived.* Payroll and pension systems seem to survive.
5. *None of the past forms of life are exactly like any of those now living.* All of the existing systems in your corporation have changed to meet the needs of the company. None are exactly the same.
6. *The two most important conditions favoring fossilization are the possession of hard parts and immediate burial.* Hard coding of information in programs encourages fossilization. Storing the code in a library and compiling the code into executable form is a way of immediately burying the changes.

All of these laws suggest that to avoid fossilization and extinction, we need to keep our software as soft and as pliable as possible. Next, let's look at various numerical laws that affect the creation and evolution of systems.

THE LAWS OF 7±2

My problem is that I have been persecuted by an integer. This number assumes a variety of disguises, being sometimes a little larger and sometimes a little smaller than usual, but never changing so much as to be unrecognizable.
                                                                    —*George A. Miller (1956)*

Even farther back in time, George A. Miller (1956) observed that the human conscious experience was like a flashlight in a darkened room that could only observe 7±2 bits of information at one time. This law can be seen in the typical phone number and many other routine groupings of people and information. Unfortunately, most customers, managers, analysts, and programmers feel that IS professionals should be able to deal with 700±200 items without any possibility of injecting defects or missing some component of the requirements. This level of complexity can be dealt with, if we chunk these software components down into chunks of 7±2 items of information, arrayed in hierarchies of 7±2 chunks. Most software engineers, however, don't bother to do this. Therefore, chaos results.

The rule of seven can be applied to everything within software development. Prototyping teams consist of 7±2 people working for 7±2 months on software systems that have 7±2 key components.

Let's begin by looking at the size and complexity of code and data. Why size and complexity? Because they directly impact the cost and schedule of software evolution. There are a number of software metrics that can be used for module size and complexity. Size can be measured by lines of code in its various forms and Halstead's Software Science metrics (Arthur 1985). McCabe's cyclomatic complexity (CC) (1976) measures the number of decision paths through the code. It can be easily calculated by adding the number of decisions (IF, CASE, WHILE, UNTIL) to the number of connectors (AND, OR, NOT) and adding one:

CC = number of decisions + number of connectors + 1

Modules approach zero defects when CC is less than 10 (i.e., 7±2). One study of Pascal and Fortran programs (Lind and Vairavan 1989) found that a CC between 10–15 minimized the number of changes (Figure 2.1). Although slightly higher than our target value of 7±2, the range obviously decreases the amount of change. Notice also that smaller values incur the highest rate of change and that the amount of change increases once CC exceeds the target value. From this we can draw our next natural law.

First Law of Complexity

McCabe's CC for any given module should be no more or less than 7±2.

Modules within the target range of 7±2 are typically defect-free, easy to maintain and enhance, and *reusable*. But how complex is too complex, you might ask. Well, Capers Jones, at his in-house conference, said that once a module exceeds a CC of 50 ($\sim 7^2$), it becomes unmaintainable and untestable. My experience suggests that Capers is absolutely correct.

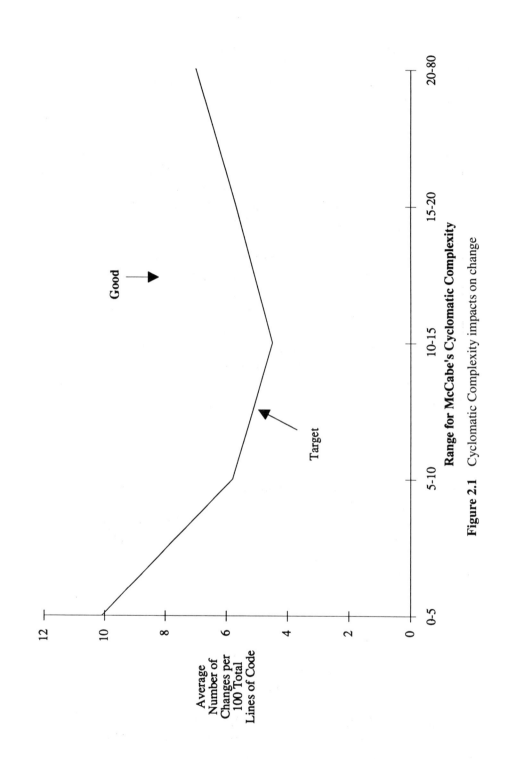

Figure 2.1 Cyclomatic Complexity impacts on change

CC isn't the only available target metric. Size, as measured by lines of code, offer other acceptable ranges:

- 25–80 executable lines of code
- 50–160 noncommentary lines of code

The same study (Lind and Vairavan 1989) contained data about the size in total lines of code (TLOC) and noncommentary source lines (NCSL). Another observation would be that for every decision, there should only be 7±2 statements contained within it, giving us a target value for executable lines of code (ELOC) of 7 decisions times 7 statements for a value of approximately 50. I can still hear the words of Ed Yourdon from a 1975 speech when he said that no module should exceed 50 statements.

The benefits of creating and maintaining small modules around these targets was confirmed by DeMarco (1989) and Lind and Vairavan (1989). This brings us to the next natural law.

First Law of Module Size

Module size in ELOC should be no more than $(7\pm2)^2$ or approximately 25–80 ELOC.

Since there should also be no more or less than 7±2 data structures containing no more or less than 7±2 data elements (Figures 2.2 and 2.3), we can further expand this law to include data and executable lines.

Second Law of Module Size

Module size in NCSL, which includes both executable and data lines, should be no more than $2*(7\pm2)^2$ or 50–160 NCSL.

Figure 2.4 shows how defect levels increase as module size continues to increase (Gaffney 1984). These examples illustrate a further natural law of software engineering. There is a target value for software components that will ensure top human performance.

The Taguchi *loss function* best describes this phenomenon. Taguchi originally developed the loss function to describe how variation in manufacturing defects caused a ''loss to society'' based on the distance from the target value. Figure 2.5 shows the upper and lower specification limits for manufactured products and the waste and rework associated with each. Manufacturing used to treat each of these categories as only having a single cost. Taguchi, however, discovered that as manufactured products trended away from the target value, there was an ever increasing associated

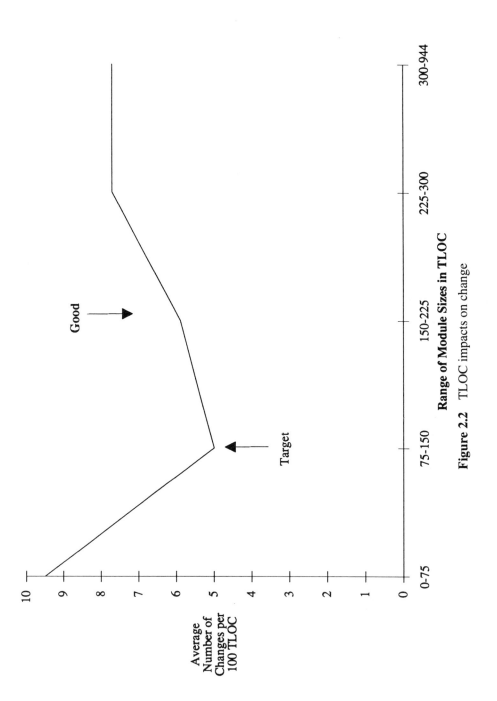

Figure 2.2 TLOC impacts on change

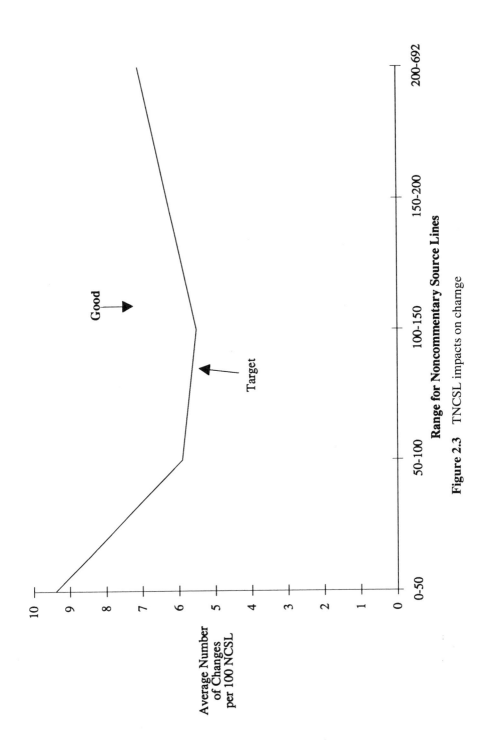

Figure 2.3 TNCSL impacts on change

45

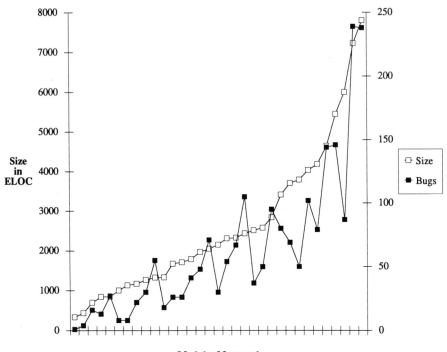

Figure 2.4   Size Impacts on Defects

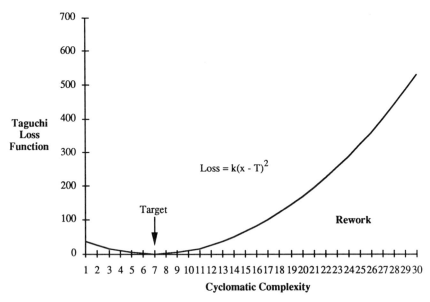

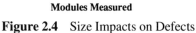

Figure 2.5   Taguchi Loss Function

cost. The function is parabolic—the farther away from the target the higher the cost. Using T as the target, x as the distance from the target, and k as a constant that can be calculated from actual costs:

$$\text{Loss} = k\ (x - T)^2$$

The constant k, at a loaded programmer rate of $120,000, is approximately $65.

Figure 2.6 shows data about lines of code (LOC) that illustrates the parabola in an Ada project. You might ask why the curve flattens out at a certain size. I don't have any data to support this, but I believe that it is because we have exceeded the human ability to understand, enhance, or test the product. That is, testers just give up after finding a certain number of bugs in a program.

I first recommended these laws of size and complexity in (Arthur 1985) and since then I have received a couple of calls a year from project managers who have tried it and come in on schedule and under budget. I attribute this to the robustness and flexibility afforded by smaller modules. These limits can be applied to testing as well:

- **First Law of Testability**

    Testable modules have 7±2 decisions and 25–100 executable statements.

- **Second Law of Testability**

    Untestable modules have 7^2 decisions (~50) and 7^4 statements (~2400).

There are, of course, other influences on complexity. Nested decisions, wide control structures, and complex documentation also influence complexity.

- **The Law of Nested Decisions**

    Nest decisions no more than three deep without chunking down and creating another module.

Now, you might ask why only three levels. My answer is that each level multiplies the complexity (e.g., one level = 1, two levels = 1*2 = 2, three

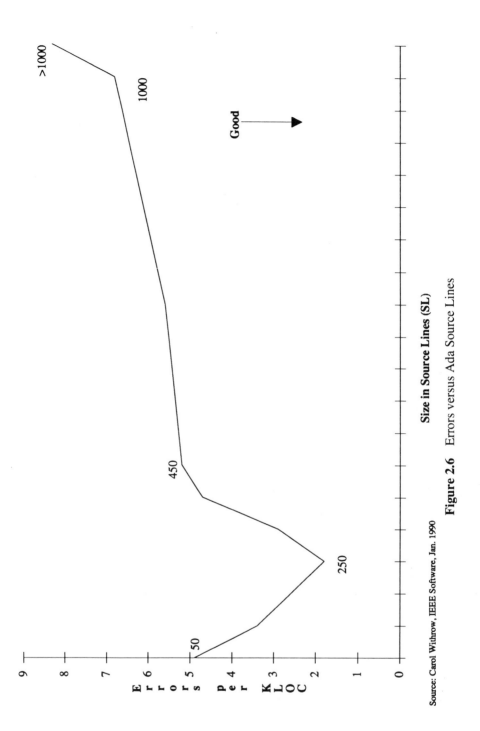

Size in Source Lines (SL)

Figure 2.6 Errors versus Ada Source Lines

Source: Carol Withrow, IEEE Software, Jan. 1990

48

levels = 1*2*3 = 6). These are called factorials (e.g., 3! = 6 which is within our range of 7±2).

- **The Law of Span of Control**

A module should directly control no more than five to nine others.

- **First Law of Documentation**

Chunk everything down into 7±2 components.

For example, consider having only seven steps in a process and seven elements in each step. When documenting a system design, have only seven elements in any given level of a data flow diagram.

The Taguchi loss function tells us that reducing the variation among programs, modules, and data will increase quality and productivity to their maximum. We can, however, exceed these limits to meet system objectives even though it incurs additional cost. Once you know the rules, you can decide how to break them creatively. Next, let's look at a law that can focus our effort.

THE LAWS OF PARETO

If you haven't already noticed, software phenomena follow a Pareto distribution (80/20). Software evolution or maintenance consumes 80 percent of your budget, while development devours the remaining 20 percent. This was also observed by Boehm (1987):

20 percent of the . . .		80 percent of the . . .
Modules	Consume	Resources
	Contribute	Errors
	Consume	Execution time
Errors	Consume	Repair costs
Enhancements	Consume	Adaptive maintenance costs
Tools	Experience	Tool usage

The Law of Pareto focuses on the 20 percent that will do you the most good.

RECENT DEVELOPMENTS

Now we can begin to look at more recent laws of software engineering.

The Laws of Requisite Simplicity

A complex system that works will invariably be found to have evolved from a simple system that works. A complex system built from scratch never works and cannot be patched up to make it work. It will have to be scrapped and redeveloped, beginning with a simple system that works. Prototyping is an excellent way to create a simple system that works. From this, all things are possible.

Newton's Law of Software

For every input, there is an equal and opposite output.

The Law of Requisite Variety

If what you're doing isn't working, try *anything* else.

LAWS OF REUSE

In *The Richest Man in Babylon,* Clason (1955) describes the secrets of wealth. His laws of accumulating wealth can be transformed to support the reuse of software.

A part of all your code is yours to keep. Code and data are acquired from the sweat of the programmer's brow and a wise programmer always creates some modules or data that can be reused in later projects. These reusable components can then become servants of the programmer to perform even greater tasks, quickly and effectively.

Start thy software repository to fattening. For every ten modules you create, use at least one to fund your reusability investments. Otherwise, day-to-day urgency will always exceed your ability to meet the needs of the future. Eric Sumner, Vice President of operations planning at AT&T Bell Labs called reusable modules "capital." Software designs, code, and data are the capital all prototyping organizations need to cut the development time dramatically.

Make thy software multiply. By coupling one reusable component together with data and other reusable components, the value of the parts increases without any additional work. Anyone who has worked with UNIX and Shell programming has experienced how one of the hundreds of tools can be coupled with others and data to increase the power of people.

Protect thy treasures from loss. Invest in a software repository (bank) and people to manage the assets it contains. Reuse must be managed. When software is loaned to a project, repository managers must keep track of where the asset has been loaned so that updates can be forwarded. And, repository managers should demand repayment in kind for reusable components; projects should repay reuse with new reusable parts. The repository staff must also accept deposits from shrewd investors seeking a good return. Some companies pay their programmers interest on reusable software components. GTE, for example, pays $50 for instances of reuse by other projects.

Increase thy ability to develop reusable software. By planning and creating reusable software, prototypers learn strategies for successful reuse. By checking what worked and what didn't using PDCA, prototypers can take continuous action to improve the kinds and quality of reusable components delivered. Some early attempts may need to be salvaged or rewritten, but over time easily reusable parts, components, and subsystems will begin to evolve to create a steady income stream—software wealth.

The first law of reuse. Productivity comes easily to the prototyper who will create and invest not less than one-tenth of his or her designs, code, and data in a reuse repository.

The second law of reuse. Reusable software labors diligently for the wise owner who finds profitable employment for it in other systems and applications.

The third law of reuse. Reusable software clings to the owner who keeps it simple and flexible. Reusable software slips away from the owner who changes it at the slightest whim or allows it to grow in all directions. Reusable software flees the prototyper who would force it to impossible performance or who follows the alluring advice of tricksters and schemers (i.e., vendors).

The fourth law of reuse. Don't solve any problem that has already been solved, especially when it's been solved by someone else who did it a whole lot more elegantly.

LAWS OF QUALITY

- Better a little caution than a great regret.
- If it ain't broke, fix it anyway (because there's always a problem or a better way to do things).
- If you use the same recipe, you'll get the same product. If you don't

improve your methodology, you'll deliver the same software with the same problems as you did last year.

LAWS OF ORGANIZATION AND STAFFING

- There is a 10:1 difference in performance between people within an organization.
- There is a 10:1 difference in performance between organizations (DeMarco and Lister, 1987).
- Eat the elephant one bite at a time.
- The power of two. Use small teams of 2–3 people for each bite.

The principle is not a thing. Call it zero.
The principle in action is the unity of creation.
This unity is a single whole. Call it one.
Creation consists of pairs of opposites or polarities. Call these polarities or pairs twos.
These polarities become creative when they interact. Their interaction is the third element. Call it three.

— John Heider
The Tao of Leadership

The power of any group is equal to the square of the number of members, divided by the number of communication paths:

$$\frac{n^2}{\frac{n(n-1)}{2}} = \frac{2n}{(n-1)}$$

Use Hired Guns

Bell Labs hires people with advanced degrees, puts them in enclosed two person offices, and empowers them to do creative work. Result: one patent a day and recognition as a world class organization.

Continuously invest in your human capital. Capers Jones suggests 15 days of training or more per year to put you in the top quartile. Tom Peters says that when you're in trouble, do more training, not less. Motorola, 1988 winner of the Malcolm Baldrige award for quality, is shooting for one month of training per employee per year.

SOFTWARE MANAGEMENT

- Managers do things right.
- Leaders do the right things.
- Great leaders do the right things right.

Natural Selection

There's always time to do the *right* projects, but there's never time to do them over.

How you manage + what you reward = the results you get

WORK ENVIRONMENT

Minimize interruptions. Ed Bliss, noted time management consultant, says: "the worst time management problem is interruptions" (1983). DeMarco and Lister found that in the top 25 percent of IS departments they evaluated, workers had 75–100 sq. ft. of *enclosed* work area and 30 sq. ft. of work surface.

Choose your weapons to match the war.

—*Bruce Cox*

The Law of Software Freshness

Automating a poor process seals in the decay as well as the goodness.

SUMMARY

Software systems created within the bounds of these natural laws will be flexible and extensible at lower cost. Doing the "right" projects—the vital few instead of the trivial many—will be more important than how you do them. Doing the right projects right (i.e., using the natural laws of software engineering) will encourage success. A good process will minimize defects and maximize flexibility. In addition, a good process will work well regardless of the technology. If technology is chosen to match the process and the project, it will encourage productivity and quality.

The moment we stop grasping for silver bullets and embrace these natural laws, software will begin to flow effortlessly from our software engineers.

CHAPTER 3

Rapid Evolutionary Development

Do it badly, do it quickly, make it better, and then say you planned it.
—Tom Peters

In the Christian ethic, everything began with Genesis. God created the world in six days and rested on the seventh. Everything else occurred through evolution. Genesis is an excellent model for rapid evolutionary development because we want to create a deliverable, functioning prototype in as short an amount of time as possible, take a deep breath, and begin the endless series of additions, changes, and deletions required to keep the system in balance and evolving to meet the needs of the business.

Notice that in Genesis, God didn't create a prototype, show it to the users, and then tell them that they would have to wait 15 million years for the real thing. God created the basic working model which contained largely pairs of opposites—heaven and earth, ground and water, light and dark, man and woman—which provided balance. God obviously had a very binary mind.

We should focus on solutions that will bear fruit quickly, within a manager's
12-month planning horizon.
—Brad Cox (1990)

Rapid evolutionary development relies on speed, simplicity, and a shared vision to create a desired product. In rapid evolutionary development, prototypers create a basic working system which does not contain all of the infinite variety the customer ultimately desires, but which does work and provides the essential initial elements of the system. To continue the organic analogy, a baby has all the bones, muscles, and organs it will ever need, but none are full sized or fully developed. Once this basic working system is installed and turned over to the customer, a series of step-wise improvements—evolutions—turn the system into the customer's desired Garden of Eden. Sounds like a utopian fantasy, doesn't it? It's much more likely to occur this way than through construction. Can you imagine what would have happened if God had tried to specify the requirements for this earthship and then build it from scratch, with all the bells and whistles? It would take 150 million years just to get started. Instead, God chose to rapid prototype the initial version in six days and grow it from there.

Rapid evolutionary development flies in the face of almost everything we believe about setting and achieving goals and objectives. It demands that we embed the decision making and direction setting in the fabric of the ongoing processes of creation and evolution. Paul MacCready, inventor of the ultralight Gossamer Condor aircraft, put it this way (Insight 1990): "If it's worth doing, it's worth doing badly. If you can make it crudely, you can make it fast and it doesn't cost much. You can test it easily . . . fix it crudely." He insists that this approach maximizes the speed of learning, and I agree; the same applies to software. We can create software quickly, learning as we go, converging on the best possible solution in record time.

Unlike the traditional development life cycle, speed is required more than direction. Once you're rolling, you can change course at will. If you're not moving, you have no feedback to guide your first steps. For those of you who know how to ski or who have thought of learning, you can't position or turn the skis until you are moving. The faster you move, the *easier* it is to turn. At too slow a speed, skis are rigid and inflexible and it takes lots of work to direct them anywhere. Like skiing, rapid evolutionary development requires that we point our skis downhill and build up some momentum before we start setting directions and goals.

BENEFITS

Compared to standard development processes, rapid evolutionary development offers several benefits. They include:

1. Achieving more effective communication because prototypes demonstrate what is happening, rather than represent it. Designs

are maps of the world; prototypes are the territory. Prototyping simplifies demonstration, evaluation, and modification of the growing system.

2. Reducing risk by eliminating uncertainty. The initial system is often created with fewer people in less time. Cycle time to proof of concept is dramatically reduced.

3. Increasing the ability to deliver *desired* functionality. Customers continuously refine their needs by using the prototype and offering feedback. This reduces the need for maintenance and enhancement when the system is delivered.

4. Incorporating a learning process into the development process. Since we know that we are operating on *incomplete knowledge* whenever we start a development process, rapid evolutionary development encourages us to learn as we go, backtracking and changing things until we get them right. It encourages rather than stifles change. Frozen requirements cannot reflect the dynamics of the organization or market.

5. Encouraging discovery and serendipity in the development of desired functionality. If we learn as we go, there is a much greater chance of discovering opportunities along the way that will shape the course of the system and possibly the course of the company.

6. Chopping cycle time from concept to delivered product by a factor of four or more. Since we are only creating the 20 percent of the product that provides 80 percent of the value, the infant system comes into the world with incredible capabilities. ''80/20 solutions . . . have a great deal to recommend them—80 percent of the ideal result, achieved through *20 percent of the effort* that might have been expended. Companies can gain strategic advantage . . . through 80/20 solutions, when aggressive company-wide efforts are judged to take too long and cost too much'' (Ernst & Young 1989).

   Evolution then expands and enhances these capabilities to quickly converge on the desired solution, even though we couldn't see it when we began the journey. Rapid evolutionary development allows information systems to be created quickly and effectively at low cost. Kraushaar (1985) suggests that the cost of a microbased system can be as low as $10,000–50,000 for a 3–12 month effort. It also permits early availability of a working system to begin exploiting the opportunities in the market.

7. Reducing defects through continuous testing and evaluation of sys-

tem components during the initial prototyping and ongoing evolutionary phases. User manuals and training can be developed *using* the working prototype to ensure accuracy.

8. Encouraging the creation of evolutionary systems that are easy to maintain because every step of development is an evolutionary step as well.

9. Continuously involving users in the solution that encourages ownership and commitment, and a level of cooperation rarely experienced. It also encourages product acceptance. The marriage of IS and users creates a healthy environment for the system's growth and development.

The "objective" is to nudge forward the process of discovering *goals along the way to induce the largest number of people possible to quickly engage, to try* something; *to maximize the odds of serendipity.*

—Tom Peters

Peters (1990) further suggested that " 'having goals' and 'making plans' are two of the most important pretenses." But they are dangerous in that they prevent us from getting into the thick of things and discovering the "real goals" and needs of our customer. Our customers don't often know for sure what they want, specifically, but they know it when they see it. Our job is to help them discover what they're really after as quickly as possible.

In Davis (1988), the authors observed that user needs are always changing and that software, by nature, is always late and falls short of the user's expectations. Evolutionary prototyping, however, minimizes delay and shortfall when compared with conventional, incremental, or throw-away prototype development approaches.

Attempts to establish software factories have often failed, largely due to a failure to understand the nature of the methods and tools required. In many cases, software factories need a toolsmith to create the tools and bridges to support the team. In others, managers mistakenly believed that their staff didn't want to change, when what the staff really wanted was to clearly understand the new process and tools. Managers often tend to view new methods and tools as a quick fix, but fail to train their personnel in even the basics of using the methods and tools. Most managers are looking for microwave solutions, not the kind of steadfast, consistent attention to training and evolution required to create an environment that fosters rapid evolutionary development.

Effective evolution of the software development process across an IS organization requires sustained management attention. Where the Hawthorne effect can create some initial improvement using CASE tools and new methods, it can take years to bring about the complete cultural shift required to make rapid evolutionary development a way of life. Yet management continues to be seduced by the siren call of vendor-promised solutions to complex problems.

What upsets software professionals more than anything is to have some new laborious paperwork process foisted on them in the guise of a great new methodology. Rapid evolutionary development, however, tends to minimize paperwork because the system grows organically. Rigorously documenting a changing structure and functionality is unnecessary. There are so few people involved in the project that communication of changes can be handled informally. Only the bare essentials of documentation are required. The prototyping team should create its own standards for depth of documentation and then follow them.

CRITICAL SUCCESS FACTORS

In Rockart and DeLong (1988), the authors describe the critical success factors of an executive support system (ESS), which, oddly enough, are also the essence of succeeding at rapid evolutionary development:

1. A committed and informed executive sponsor
2. An operating sponsor—a champion
3. Appropriate IS staff
4. Appropriate technology
5. Management of data
6. A clear link to business objectives
7. Management of organizational resistance
8. Management of system evolution and spread

At Hitachi (Cusumano 1989), management found that it needed: a disciplined and standardized approach to development, an effective way to visualize and control the production process, a consistent way to specify requirements, an integrated set of tools, portable computer languages, and reuse of components. Rapid evolutionary development encompasses all of these things.

We could talk at length about these critical success factors, but I think they speak for themselves. Next, an organization must put aside its internal struggles for power and focus on the ecology of the whole organism to:

1. Identify the most strategic application required
2. Create and grow the application to the desired level
3. Evolve the application to maximize its benefits and sustain competitive advantage

The executive sponsor can help manage the internal battles for funding and systems, and provide help prioritizing the applications to be completed. The first application chosen for rapid development should be of medium priority and then as the prototyping teams develop the skills to handle increasingly complex projects, the applications selected should be ones that can influence the corporation's survival or dramatically impact the bottom line. Once a project is chosen, the prototyping team can begin working with the customer to create the first working version of the system which is then delivered into production. From there, the prototyping team can continue to grow and evolve the system toward the customer's desired solution. In essence, the system continues to grow indefinitely unless an innovation occurs that pushes it onto a dying branch of the evolutionary tree.

RAPID EVOLUTIONARY DEVELOPMENT

Imagine walking into a car dealer's showroom and seeing that perfect red sports car that you've always wanted. The salesperson takes you for a test drive and it feels like a dream. It corners like it's on rails and the acceleration is second to none. You know that in this car, you'll feel unstoppable. This car is everything you've ever wanted. You say, "I'll take one" and the salesperson says, "I'm sorry . . . this is only a prototype, but I can have one ready for you in 24–36 months." How would you feel? Disappointed? Angry? Would you take your business elsewhere?

This is the common mistake most prototyping projects make using the construction paradigm. They believe that the customer will stand still, waiting while the IS staff redevelops the "production" version of the system based on the prototype's demonstrated requirements. If you can show it to them, they'll want it and you had better be ready to deliver, or there will be hell to pay in terms of customer relations and lost credibility.

If you are going to create a prototype, it must be a deliverable prototype that can then be evolved to meet the customer's desires and expectations. It is much easier to manage the momentum of a system in operation than it is to shout *"Stop!"* when the prototype is completed and start building the production system.

One way to look at rapid evolutionary development would use a logical view of what happens:

Grow (initial prototype)**Creation**
Until (replaced)**Evolution**
    Grow (expanded version)
enduntil

Grow (system)
    Until (converge to a solution)
        (Plan) Analyze the customer's needs
           • people, tools, environment
           • processes
        (Do) Create a demonstrable prototype
        Check closeness of fit
        Act to improve
    enduntil
    Deliver the system
End (Grow)

First, we create and grow the initial working system. Then, until the system is replaced by a younger one, we continue to expand and grow the system from infancy to maturity using PDCA. Amazing things can happen using this approach.

"At DuPont, the use of an iterative development approach, coupled with heavy user involvement and CASE tools, has produced more than 400 new programs with no failures and helped reduce maintenance by 70 to 90 percent."

"TransWorld Airlines Inc. completely rewrote its IMS-based frequent flier program in a relational database system. The project took 15 months using a data driven methodology and integrated CASE tools. Users can now add new functions to the application in four to eight hours. In isolated cases, users reported fivefold productivity gains in new product development" (Moad 1990).

Despite the success stories, few IS organizations have undertaken the job of transforming the development and maintenance processes to one of an evolutionary nature.

Another way to look at rapid evolutionary development is being like human courtship and family development.

Courtship

You have to choose the right mate. Initially, there's a lot of courting as the software developer and customer romance each other. Eventually, they decide to "get into bed" together. A prenuptial agreement is often a great idea.

Pregnancy

Prototyping is much like pregnancy. First, the customer conceives an idea. Together, the software developers and the customer work together as the fertile nucleus develops into the initial version of the system. This pregnancy is accompanied by tremendous enthusiasm and growth.

Notice that mothers never ask fathers "How many corners do you want me to cut in the construction of our child?" Systems with birth defects usually carry them for the rest of their life unless a highly skilled software surgeon makes the necessary repairs. Lots of prenatal care will prevent such problems.

Also notice that fathers never ask "How long will this take? Couldn't you deliver it in four months instead of nine?" Because everyone knows it takes nine months, no matter how many people you put on the task. Children born prematurely need a lot of care, most of it expensive. Children born too late are a burden on the mother and cause endless anxiety. It's best to let the prototyping process take its natural course and deliver the baby when it's ready.

During this period, the parents must prepare a loving environment to receive the new child. Everyone has to be trained in child care, feeding, and so on.

Birth

At birth the system is formed sufficiently to live in the world. The initial version (a small one) is "delivered" and installed for use. Like most newborns, it will wake its parents up in the middle of the night with all kinds of problems—it can soil itself, it can get sick, and it can get hungry. New systems need a lot of initial care. Parents don't say "When is this child going to be able to take care of itself?" because they know it will take time for the system to reach a level of maturity where it can do things for itself.

The Terrible Twos

The system needs a lot of care and feeding in its first few years as it continues to grow. Like expectant parents, the software developers and the customers continue to care for its needs. The rampant enthusiasm of the pregnancy yields to a feeling of confinement. A lot of preparation and work must go into any outing with the new system. The baby system continues to grow organically and naturally—no new hands, feet, or organs are added.

It is a good idea at this point to immunize the system against all of the childhood diseases.

Childhood

Look who's talking! At this point the system is fairly well mannered. It continues to grow and learn at a reasonable rate. Customers and IS both enjoy this period of working together to help the system develop.

Adolescence

The system will continue to grow, gain weight, and learn. At this stage, changes in markets or organizations can cause problems. The software may develop some wild hormonal urges that will test the mettle of the developer and customer. The software may need braces for its teeth or strong guidance to set its path.

At this point, the system may get the urge to spin off some children of its own. *Just say no!*

Adulthood

Maturity develops. We can no more create a mature system than we can create a mature person. As the system matures, however, it will provide increasingly more benefit to the customer and require less support and attention from the developer.

At some point in their life, systems may put on some extra weight and need to reduce some of the flab—both data and processes. Some systems will opt for plastic surgery and various cremes and balms to postpone the aging process. This is okay! No one likes ugly, old systems; we appreciate elegant, mature ones. Through good nutrition and balanced effort, the system can stay younger longer than we perhaps ever thought possible.

Old Age

Through proper exercise and diet, software can thrive. It can live a long and healthy life and retire, or it can develop all kinds of health problems and require expensive medical care. All of this depends on how it was treated during its lifetime. Rapid evolutionary development demands that we examine the overall ecology of any change in the system during its life.

I prefer this metaphor of courting and childbearing to the more algorithmic model offered previously. The question on your mind now, however, might be: "How do I begin to use the model?"

Process

History has shown us that large, cumbersome methodologies will only fit a certain size of project, not all projects. These heavy methodologies also generate masses of paper and require extensive paper support systems which further impede productivity.

A flexible, evolutionary prototyping methodology lays out the fundamentals of software creation and evolution using PDCA. It can significantly improve productivity and quality. The methodology works like the expansion unit in a personal computer: The application creation or evolution team can choose the specific *methods* (expansion cards) to customize the prototyping methodology to match their application.

Using a flexible methodology, we can then integrate software tools with the methods to create an integrated, *technology platform* to automate the software processes. The technology platform will then support all of the activities of software creation and evolution.

The creation process for rapid evolutionary development is simple (see Figure 3.1) and includes:

- Planning the project
- Creating the prototype
- Checking closeness of fit
- Acting to improve it

PLAN

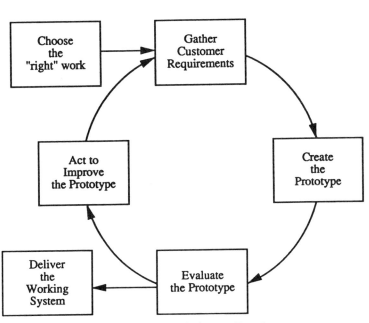

Figure 3.1   Rapid Evolutionary Development

Plan the Project

1. Choose a project which requires fast delivery and is not well understood. This means that there must be rapid growth and evolution of
   the requirements and the whole product during its development.
   Iteration and evolution will occur whether it is planned for or not.
   Planned evolution before the product escapes is better than unplanned evolution after a failure in the field.

2. Gather and define customer and market requirements. It is useful at
   this point to begin framing the user's expectations of the creation
   process. We will focus on their *needs* not their *wants* or *wishes*.
   Many rounds of mutual negotiation, participation, and feedback
   will be required to evolve the prototype to the point that it can be
   used effectively. This repeated assessment of the customer's and
   market's requirements will ensure rapid convergence on the best
   possible solution.

3. As we gather requirements, we need to begin sorting and chunking the customer's requests into needs, wants, and wishes. We need to begin anticipating the evolutionary path of the system as it grows. Process analysis helps IS guide the technical evolution. Will the system be a plant, rooted in one place, or a more mobile system that can move quickly to attack various markets?

Create the Prototype

4. Create a prototype or model. The prototype plays a key role in the success of the software mission. A demonstrable, behavioral model provides so much feedback that you can't help but come up with better products. Static, two-dimensional representations (i.e., design documents) of dynamic software systems that are supposed to move, grow, and process information cannot help but be incomplete.

Check Closeness of Fit

5. Evaluate the prototype using customer feedback. Given a working, demonstrable system, customers can tell you how far or how close you are to their goal. They can give you better feedback about how to make the system better.

Act to Improve

6. Using customer and prototyper feedback, act to improve the prototype. Identify the next steps required to ecologically grow the fetal system to the next step in its evolution.

Deliver the Prototype

Once the prototype has grown and evolved to a level that can support the customer's vital requirements, it can be delivered for use. Then, like all living systems, it will continue to grow in size and skill for many years.

SOFTWARE EVOLUTION

Unlike a car that rolls off an assembly line or a house ready for occupancy, software systems continue to expand and change over time. The next step of rapid evolutionary development delivers the system into everyday use. From here on, the freewheeling accelerated growth of the prenatal system slows. The system grows and evolves in a more carefully orchestrated and focused process of software evolution (Arthur 1988).

The software creation process (steps 1–6) can be used throughout the system's life to create major enhancements and extensions of the system's knowledge and abilities. Using the software evolution process (see Chapter 8) and the rapid evolutionary development process, prototypers can continuously improve and enhance the system as the environment changes around it. The system, however, is not the only thing that needs to evolve.

Evolution of the Methodology

One of the problems with most construction or manufacturing methodologies is that they rarely evolve to meet the changing needs of the business or technology. When a methodology does change, it is typically too little too late. The methodology and technology must evolve to match the needs of the customer. The PDCA process described in Chapter 10 will assist you in keeping the process and technology up-to-date with the evolutionary life forms created using rapid evolutionary development.

SUMMARY

In this chapter the benefits, critical success factors, and process of rapid evolutionary development have been explored. By using the metaphor of evolution, the constraints of the construction paradigm can be dropped and new ways to quickly grow working systems that can surprise and delight both users and IS personnel can be discovered. We've also looked briefly at the other evolutionary processes that support continued growth of the software, software processes, and technology that support it. In Chapter 4, we'll look at ways to gather customer requirements in ways that allow us to focus on the vital 20 percent of the functionality that will provide 80 percent of the benefit. We'll learn how to separate customer *needs* from *wants* and *wishes*. Once their needs are known in sufficient detail, we can begin to use rapid prototyping to create systems in record time.

Right Requirements

Since the mind is a specific biocomputer, it needs specific instructions and directions.

— Denis Waitley

The power of a successfully communicated thought, from one human mind to another, is one of the most powerful forces we know.

When thought and action are combined together, however, the results are powerful.

— John-Roger and Peter McWilliams (1990)

How do I write good requirements for software? This question continues to resonate throughout the software industry. Going back to the evolutionary model of software, you can observe that it isn't possible to prespecify all of the customer's requirements. If requirements are a living, moving, changing thing, why would we want to "freeze" them? To prevent decay or to stop the growth? Probably the latter.

The customer, in their usual desire to have the best for less, will want everything yesterday and at a low cost. We often neglect to understand our users because it is so much easier to develop our "creative" ideas in a vacuum than it is to expose them to the winds of criticism and change. To counteract this tendency, begin with early and continuous focus on the user community, their needs, desires, wants, and wishes.

1. Decide who they are
2. Talk to them
3. Work with them directly at their location
4. Observe them working
5. Try their job
6. Involve them in the design

Customers have had a hard time describing their requirements for a number of reasons:

- Knowing the problem too well, which makes it hard to explain (e.g., if someone asked you how to drive a car, you would have a hard time describing it in detail, even though you know how to do it well)
- Not taking enough time to adequately discover and understand their needs
- Not knowing how to effectively communicate their needs
- Not knowing the possibilities offered by information technology

In rapid evolutionary development, customers can have *anything* they want, but not *everything* they want. The solution is preventative: You must choose carefully at the outset.

What this means is that we must begin with the customer's outcome as our primary goal. To do this, the prototyper must use the model shown in Figure 4.1. First, the prototyper must focus on the customers (people); second, on their needs; third, on organizing what they have asked for into some conceptual or logical model (process); fourth, create the working prototype (technology), and, finally, check with the customer to ensure that the prototype is what they want and act to improve it if it isn't. In following this process, the prototyper uses the PDCA life cycle:

Plan   Develop rapport with the customer so that they will know that you are on their side. Using the natural human ability of observing others—sensory acuity—the prototyper can establish rapport with the customer using their physiology, voice tones, and words that match the customer's dialect. This requires flexibility on the part of the prototyper. Developing rapport before moving ahead simplifies the process of gathering information to create a good prototype.

Next, the prototyper needs to *frame* the development pro-

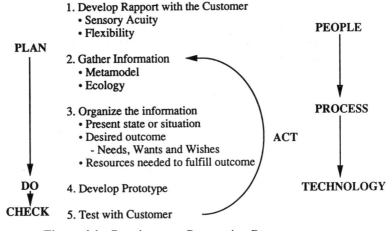

Figure 4.1 Requirements Prototyping Process

cess. Customers get upset because we don't live up to their initial expectations. By setting these expectations before we begin, the customer will be better able to understand the process. The creation process, for instance, will be fast and furious, converging quickly on a solution that embodies the critical functionality of the system. The evolution process requires a more measured approach to expand the system ecologically into the mature system the customer desires. An ounce of framing the development process is worth a pound of reframing the result.

Once the rapid evolutionary frame is established, the prototypers can begin to gather information using verbal skills called the meta-model to clarify the customer's vague needs into clear, specific ones. While gathering information, the prototyper often begins to organize the information into three different categories: present situation, desired outcome, and the existing or necessary resources needed to create the outcome. The prototyper must also separate the needs from the wants and wishes. In rapid evolutionary development, the prototype only has room for the customer's needs, not their wants and wishes. These only serve to clutter and confuse the development process with unnecessary complexity. The prototyper can capture these wants and wishes now to guide the future evolution of the system.

User requirements typically suffer from misunderstandings, ambiguities, inconsistencies, and omissions. So the prototyper must also focus on the ecological aspects of the evolving requirements—will they meet the needs of the customer and organization without harming some other part of the company? What has the customer forgotten or overlooked that could be a problem with the newly evolving system? An information system that enhances the health of one department at the expense of another is not in anyone's best interests because it will eventually need to be scrapped and replaced with one that keeps everyone's best interests in mind.

Do   Once the prototyper has gathered sufficient information about the customer's problems and needs, he can then begin to develop the prototype using the appropriate technology.

Check   With a working prototype of the customer's needs in hand, the prototyper must re-establish rapport, demonstrate the prototype, and check whether it meets his needs or not.

Act   If the prototype did not meet the customer's needs, the prototyper continues to maintain rapport and use the meta-model to gather and organize more information about how to improve the prototype.

PLAN

Notice that the focus of this process is the planning stage—customer and prototyper working hand in hand to understand each other's needs. Then the prototyper uses technology to create the prototype and returns to the customer to check and improve on the result. Prototyping projects often fail because they unleash a horde of technologists on a group of customers without regard for the human dynamics of the requirements process. The technologists, using their own particular brand of technospeak, appear to be talking *down* to the customers, instead of talking *with* them. This creates resentment, breaks rapport, and leads to frustration and anxiety. At this stage, both parties have a desire to be done with the requirements process and to leap into development. Unfortunately, jumping into the creation process leads to rapid development of the wrong product. Then some maintenance crew must deal with the associated waste and rework to sustain the genetically defective system. The human element is so important that a good deal of time will be spent on discussing how to weave people into the rapid evolutionary development equation.

People

The average programmer or systems analyst has the interpersonal skills of a professional wrestler. The analyst and customer enter the ring like two combatants with hidden agendas: The analyst seeks to maximize the use of new and interesting technology and the customer seeks to maneuver the analyst into giving them what they want at the lowest possible price. Then, they go through a series of choreographed throws and falls until one or the other manages to pin the other down long enough for the bout to be declared over. One wins, one loses and they are both physically worn out. Occasionally, additional blows are shared in the march to the locker room.

In essence, both parties are working independently toward different goals. Compare this to the fourth, fifth, and sixth habits of highly effective people (Covey 1989): think win/win; seek first to understand, *then* to be understood; and synergize. Humans often fail to observe that they are dependent on other people for everything that they receive. All the money you receive comes from other people, and the amount of money you receive is dependent on the value of the goods and services you provide to other people. Customers and technologists are *interdependent*; one cannot survive without the other. Thus, to succeed, we must think win/win in all of our negotiations.

I have seen customers demand, demand, demand, and managers drive their technologists to work harder, longer, and more stressfully to give customers what they want. This is not win/win. Similarly, I've seen people who only wanted to play with the latest technology, people who simply assumed that someone should pay them for the pleasure of pursuing their own interests. This is not win/win. More often, these two extremes create whine/whine, with both sides complaining bitterly of the other's inability to understand the intricacies and complexities of business or technology. Most often, whine/whine results from the failure of both sides to use the fifth habit: seek first to understand and then to be understood, which leads us to step 1 of Figure 4.1.

To truly create win/win relationships and solutions, the prototyper must first seek to understand the customer's needs, wants, and wishes. Understanding the customer's point of view is often impossible from the technologist's standpoint. To truly understand, we must first establish rapport with the customer and enter their world. Once we understand their map of reality, then we can lead them to understand ours.

Rapport

Successful rapid evolutionary development projects depend on the relationship between the system's parents—the customer and IS. Relationships begin by establishing rapport. If you have a good relationship with someone, it is because you have done things to establish and maintain rapport over time.

The science of rapport is startlingly simple and yet few people know anything about it. It's surprising that people ever manage to create systems. Usually when they do, however, the product fails to meet the customer's needs and the evolution staff spends the next few years bringing the product up to the customer's expectations.

Many corporations consider communication to be a major problem and it is. People are communicating all the time; the problem is that the message being sent is not being received. We're not connecting with our intended audience and our sensitivity is so low that we often ignore their response. Like some crazy person in a foreign country, we shout our message louder without changing the content and expect that to make it better understood.

Figure 4.2 shows the components of communication: physiology, tonality of voice, and words. It may surprise many of you that words are such a small component of our total communication. They are still important, but not as important as physiology and tone of voice. For example, a customer who is sitting up attentively is sending a different message than one who is slumped down in his chair tapping a pencil on the table. A customer using a caustic tone of voice is sending a different message than one whose vocal variety is balanced and melodic.

If we only listen to the words customers use, we will miss up to 93 percent of the message. Is it any wonder that the requirements *specification* process can only gather perhaps 60% of the customer's requirements?

Written documents can only capture the words, pictures, and diagrams. They cannot capture the tone of voice and behavioral demonstrations of the customer. This is why rapid prototyping is such a powerful form of requirements gathering: It connects the prototyper with the customer in ways that allow a relationship to develop. The connection facilitates communication at all levels and provides the customer with the most powerful form of feedback from the prototyper—a behavioral demonstration of the desired

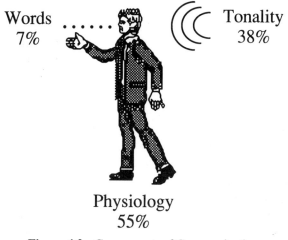

Figure 4.2 Components of Communication

outcome. No other known process can achieve these results. And it all begins with rapport.

An old adage suggests that you never get a second chance to make a first impression. The science of rapport explains this, because people like to be around people that are *like* them, not different. Is it any wonder that a technology speaking person never gets to first base with a business speaking customer? The prototyper's goal is to establish rapport with the customer the first time they meet and then to maintain and develop the relationship over time. Rapport is established or broken in the first 60 seconds of any interaction through similarities or differences in physiology, tonality, and word choice. This requires flexibility on the part of the prototyper.

Flexibility

To achieve rapport, a prototyper's first choice is to *match* or *mirror* the customer's physiology—how they are standing or sitting, how they shake hands, or how they cock their head to one side or the other. I challenge you to take the next three interactions you have with anyone and align your body or breathing to theirs and see if you don't automatically develop new levels of rapport and automatically begin moving toward win/win solutions. Do this with your spouse, children, significant other, or your pets for practice.

The number one way to establish rapport is to pace another person's breathing. Mothers and their babies breathe together for nine months. Is it any wonder that Mother's Day is more popular than Father's Day? You can see a person's breath by watching the rise and fall of their shoulders or by noticing that when they speak, they must be breathing out. Matching the customer's physiology and breath will give you 55 percent of the rapport you need to move ahead successfully.

Next, you will need to match the person's vocal variety, inflections, and words. There are three pervasive communication styles (Figure 4.3): visuals, auditories, and kinesthetics. Visuals tend to look up (this is where most people store and create pictures of their world), speak quickly, and talk in a higher pitch. They also tend to breathe in their upper chest and gesture higher than the other communication styles. Visuals like to "*see* the big picture" or "*look* at what we need." Auditories tend to look toward their left or right ear (this is where most people store and create sounds and words), speak more rhythmically, and in a more melodic tone of voice. Auditories tend to breathe and gesture near the midline of their bodies. Auditories say things like "that *sounds* good to me" or "that *clicks* for me" or "that *rings a bell*." Kinesthetics tend to look down and to their right (which is where most people store and access feelings), speak more slowly, and in a flat, deep voice. Kinesthetics breathe deeply, in their abdomen and gesture very little. Kinesthetics say things like "that *feels* like the right choice" or "I can *get a handle* on that" or "I'm *warming* up to the idea." They're usually hot, cold, or lukewarm about everything in their lives. Kinesthetics store information on a deep level. Thus once they get an

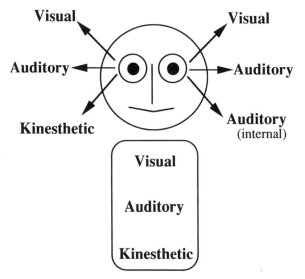

Figure 4.3 Communication Styles

idea, they've got it for life. Unfortunately, if they get the wrong idea about you or your newfangled technology, it's hard to change their mind. All the more reason to establish rapport *before* you begin prototyping.

To the extent that you can match your customer's vocal style and the words they use, you will establish further levels of rapport and understanding. Establishing and maintaining rapport with customers demands that the prototyper learn how to read the customer's physiology, tonality, and words. In industry jargon, this is known as *sensory acuity* (Figure 4.1). (I've touched briefly on how to do this. For more depth, see Laborde 1985.) Then, when you seek to be understood, you can present your message with the words, tonality, and physiology that *they* can understand.

This section on rapport has discussed a specific process for initiating respectful communication with customers to understand their needs and wants. The prototyper begins first by developing rapport through matching and mirroring the customer's physiology, vocal tone and tempo, and their choice of words. This is actually the first step of the prototyping process.

Next, the prototyper will continue the prototyping process by gathering information about the customer's requirements (step 2). Then, the prototyper must begin to organize the information (step 3) in preparation for developing the prototype (step 4) and testing it with the customer (step 5). The prototyper continues to iterate steps 1–5 until the customer approves the improved version for implementation. From there, the evolutionary process is used to transform the initial working system into its final form.

Gathering Information

There are many potential pitfalls in information gathering. There can be missing, incorrect, or excess information about:

- Functions
- Data
- Interfaces
- Performance requirements
- Quality requirements—human factors, future flexibility, and maintainability
- Bells and whistles

To be an effective prototyper, you must be able to understand your customer's model or map of the world. You must have a means of reaching into their mind to gather facts and understand how they look at the world, hear what's going on, and feel about their experience.

In the 1970s, a former computer programmer named Richard Bandler and his partner John Grindner studied two of the world's leading psychotherapists, Milton Erickson and Virginia Satir. In the process of modeling their behaviors to determine what made their changes work, Bandler and Grindner first discovered these therapists' rapport skills. Next, they discovered that Erickson and Satir spent a significant amount of time gathering information. To do so, they used specific techniques that clarified the patient's needs and wants to crystal clarity (or razor sharpness depending on your communication style). These techniques were later to become known as the *meta-model*. As Erickson and Satir used the meta-model to clarify a patient's requirements, they also checked the ecology of their choices. For example, patients might say that they wanted freedom in *every* part of their lives, but there are laws and relationships that bind us and even the physical limitation of the planet. The therapist had to narrow the patients' outcome to focus on those areas where freedom to choose would not harm them or others.

And this is exactly what a prototyper or requirements developer does with a customer. A prototyper extracts the customer's needs, wants, and wishes into a clear, achievable outcome that can be turned into a working prototype. The ability to gather this information to successfully develop a product that meets the customer's requirements depends on the proto-typer's ability to establish rapport and use the meta-model.

Meta-Model

> *No matter what sound-making device is placed at their disposal, creatures in general do a great deal of gabbling, and it requires long patience and observation to edit out the parts lacking syntax and sense. Light social conversation, designed to keep the party going, prevails. Nature abhors a long silence.*
> — *Lewis Thomas (1975)*

The meta-model (Table 4.1) recognizes that customers will do a lot of gabbling and that somewhere, buried in the midst of that noise, are the customer's requirements. The trick is to have the patience, tenacity, and sensory acuity to identify those parts and extract them into a useful description that can initiate the creation and evolution of the application prototype. The meta-model assumes that the customer will communicate obscurely in three ways: generalizations, deletions, and distortions. The meta-model further assumes that no two human neurologies are the same and that to

TABLE 4.1   Neuro-Linguistic Programming Meta-Model

Type	Violation	Response
General-ization	**Universal Quantifiers** Always, every, never	Exaggerate! *Always? Every? Never?*
	Judgments Right, wrong, good, bad	Bad *for whom?*
Deletion	**Verb–nouns** I need more information	Use the verb or noun in a question How would you like to be informed? Where? When? What kind?
	Unspecified Nouns He, she, they, no one, it, people, problems, data	Who, specifically? What, specifically?
	Adjectives without a noun She's the best	How or What, Specifically? How was she the best, specifically? What was she the best at doing?
	Unspecified Verbs All verbs: He kicked me	How, specifically? Where, specifically?
	Operators of Necessity, **Possibility, Impossibility** Should, shouldn't, ought to, must, have to	What would happen if? What causes you to . . . or prevents you from . . . ? What would happen if you did/didn't? What stops you?
	could, would, want, can't, impossible, unable	If we could do that, would you want it? What stops/prevents you?
Distortion	**Cause and Effect** Makes, forces, causes Computers make me crazy	How does X make you Y? How do computers make you crazy?
	Mind Reading I know what's best for them.	How, specifically, do you know that?

understand customers clearly, we must investigate, investigate, investigate, until a clear map of their needs can be drawn.

Generalizations take the form of statements that include the words: *every, all, always,* and *never.* "We *always* process the billing information this way." Or, "We *never* use account information to evaluate marketing strategies." Generalizations like these are extremely dangerous and often tell a lot about the limits of the customer's perception of their job. Many times, through more thorough examination of these generalizations, the prototyper can discover unmet needs and desires that, when automated, will create a new level of trust and devotion in the customer. The way we explore these generalizations is through the meta-model.

I keep six honest serving men
(They taught me all I knew)
Their names are What and Why and When
And How and Where and Who.

— Rudyard Kipling

To respond to generalizations, we exaggerate them by accentuating the key words and their implications: "You *always* process the billing information this way? There are no exceptions? No ways to do it better?" Or, "You *never* evaluate marketing strategies with existing account information? What do you use? Witchcraft? Oracles? Gut feel? *What would happen if* you could use that information to understand your markets in ways that you never thought possible?"

Another form of generalization is a judgment: *right, wrong, good,* or *bad.* A customer, for example, might say, "This is the right way to handle a voucher." The prototyper's response would be, "Right *for whom?*" or "According to whom?" Or the customer might say, "That's wrong." Again, the response would be "Wrong *for whom?*" These kinds of binary judgments often overlook the vital exceptions that are necessary to build a flexible, robust system. They also show the prototyper the boundaries of the customer's map of the world. Will users sail off the end of the world if they change the way they think about these judgments, or, like Columbus, will they discover new worlds and new markets?

Another form of requirements fog is deletions and these are perhaps the most insidious of requirements flaws. When the customer fails to describe something, it's often overlooked until much later in the development process. Then they whine and cajole until we agree to put it in (at great expense and rework), but they seem to forget that it wasn't part of the original deal. Schedules slip, tempers flare, and credibility goes down the toilet.

Deletions account for much of the vast missing portion of a customer's requirements. Customers don't go out of their way to delete information. They do so by using vague nouns and verbs that are the foundation of most hypnotic language (called the Milton model). Vague words allow the prototyper to draw their own pictures, sounds, and feelings about what the customer wants. Unfortunately, a prototyper's and customer's world are usually light years apart.

One of the most common forms of deletions is processes that have been turned into objects—verbs that have been turned into nouns (nominalization). The word deletion, for example, is a nominalization: the verb *delete* has been turned into an object that is missing. Nominalizations often obscure the very information a prototyper needs to successfully create the product. For another example, take the word freedom. For one person, freedom may mean financial freedom, for another, the freedom to travel, for another, the freedom to change jobs. Freedom is another verb that has been transformed into a noun. Where requirements developers go wrong is by taking a deletion such as freedom and applying it to *their* map of reality, not the customer's.

To begin to clarify the customer's needs, the prototyper would need to transform the noun back into a verb: "How would you like to be free, specifically?" Or, "What, specifically, would free you now?" Another common example would be if an executive customer said, "I'd like more information." The prototyper could ask about the unspecified noun or the verb: "Could you be more specific about *what* you would like to know more about?" Or, "*How* would you like to be better informed, specifically?" These forms of deletions, decision (decide), information (inform), freedom (free), and so on, are so common that we often overlook them in normal language patterns. The prototyper can also treat these nominalizations as unspecified verbs or nouns.

Nominalizations and words such as *he, she, they,* or *it* are unspecified nouns—another form of deletion. Prototypers would respond by gathering more data by asking "Who or What, specifically?" If the customer said, "I'd like more information," the prototyper could respond with, "*What* kind of information, *specifically?*" If the customer said, "*They*'re *always* sending the *wrong* information!" the prototyper could respond by asking, "*Who, specifically*, sends you the *wrong* information. Is it *always* wrong and how is it wrong, specifically? Isn't there anyone who needs this information?" Or a customer might say, "I'd like a report." To which you might reply, "Of what? How often? Who else should receive this report? How would you like to receive it?" And so on.

Adjectives are another form of deletion. Typically, the noun modified by the adjective has been deleted: "The old system was better!" Better at what? In what way? How, specifically? Other comparative adjectives include: *more, less, better, higher, lower, closer, down,* or *up,* and most words that end in *-er.*

Unspecified verbs are another form of deletion and virtually all verbs are vague in some sense. For example, "We send the order to purchasing." How do you send it? "We mail it." How do you mail it? "We put the P.O. in an intracompany envelope and put it in the outgoing company mail." And so on. Or the customer might say, "I'd like to print the data." The prototyper would respond, "How, specifically?" The answers received can vary widely: "On the screen" or "On the laser printer" or "On microfiche."

Words such as *should, shouldn't, must,* and *have to* also show the boundaries of the customer's map of reality. The "modal operators of necessity" tell us what customers believe they have to do or not do. In reply to these words, the prototyper can ask: "What would happen if you did or didn't?" For example, the customer might say, "We *must* produce these figures on a quarterly basis." The prototyper replies, "What would happen if you didn't?" The customer might say, "Oh, not much, I guess," implying that this is more of a want than a requirement for the initial system. Or the customer might say, "The IRS will be down our throats for tax evasion," implying absolute necessity. These words, especially *must,* often imply an absolute requirement for the system being built. This is how the prototyper can tell the 20 percent that gives 80 percent of the benefit apart from the rest of the customer's babblings. Compare these operators of necessity with operators of possibility *could, would, want,* and *wish* that imply the customer's wants, but not necessarily needs. You could test their importance easily by asking "What would happen if we postponed these into future versions?" These are the other 80 percent of the system's requirements that should be noted for the future evolutionary effort.

The customer may also use words that imply impossibility: *can't, unable, impossible,* or *no way.* The customer might say, "We can't access stock level records." To which, the prototyper would reply, "What stops you?" or "What would happen if you could?" These key words are another great opportunity to open up the horizons of the customer's model and provide much greater value in the delivered system. Overcoming impossibilities can easily take the system and the company in new directions that can ensure their survival.

A *distortion* is the other type of communication problem. A distortion takes seemingly real requirements and distorts them. There are two types of distortions: cause and effect, and mind reading.

Cause and effect statements assume that one thing causes another to happen. For example, "When accounts update the bank transactions, it makes the system slow." This presupposes that updates of bank transactions cause the system to be slow. This may or may not be true. To accept such a statement as fact can lead a prototyper astray. The prototyper's response could be, "How do banking transaction updates make the system slow?" Customers will either clarify their arguments or abandon them. Continue to gather more information using the meta-model to ensure that they know what they're talking about.

Mind reading presupposes that one person can know what another is thinking and that is what has gotten software developers in trouble before. For example, if a customer says, "I know the boss would like it like this," he is implying that he knows what the boss wants. The prototyper can test this assertion for validity: "How do you know that, specifically?" The answers you get will surprise you.

A word of caution: Continuous use of the meta-model can alienate your users. Question after question can drive people crazy quickly. To maintain rapport, you will need to soften your approach using backtracking and softeners. When you backtrack, you simply repeat back to the users what you thought they said in answer to your question. You can repeat it directly, to build rapport, or you can paraphrase it to help ensure understanding:

Customer: I want a weekly report of account information.

Prototyper: So, what you're telling me is that you want a *weekly* report of account information. What account information would you like to receive, specifically?

or

Prototyper: So you would like a weekly report about your accounts. How would you like to be informed, in a printed report or by selecting the data from a screen? What account information would you like, specifically?

Backtracking maintains and builds rapport so that you can ask the next question. Other softeners can be added at the beginning of your question:

> Prototyper: I was wondering what kind of account information you would like in the weekly report. Would you prefer to have the account information printed and distributed to you, or would you rather get it from the system on-line?

Softening the questions helps maintain your connection with your customer. Otherwise, it's easy to seem too probing. Data gathering can become an inquisition which can lead to a breakdown in communications.

I saw a blatant example of missed communications when I worked at Bell Labs. Fourteen Bell operating companies had asked for some radical changes in a report we produced. The report controlled all kinds of major construction activities, and every time the report was produced, the figures would change due to changing volumes of telephone traffic. The analyst who took the requirements decided, based on his map of reality, that the users were asking for two more reports: one that showed the differences between the old report and the new one, and another that showed both the old and the new together, neither of which was the actual requirement. As it turned out, users were spending a lot of time checking the new report against the old, and wherever the difference between the old and new value was less than some limit, they were penciling in the old amount. This prevented the development of construction plans where there wasn't enough change to make the construction feasible.

What the customer really wanted was for the report program to compare the old and the new values, and then to reset the values that were less than the threshold. It took almost two years to develop the first enhancement only to discover that it was a great solution to the *wrong* problem, from the customer's point of view.

Thus, as you can notice from these examples, there are many ways to overlook or miss the very data you need to create a prototype or evolutionary change that will meet the customer's needs. As you continue on your day-to-day activities and as you listen to others speak, you will begin to notice the trigger words discussed in this section and automatically begin to question their meaning. And as you discover more about these words and their ability to derail a development effort, you will find yourself using Kipling's serving men more and more to keep your creation on track.

Notice, however, that I left off one of Kipling's serving men: *why. Why* questions are the endless loop questions of life: Why did that happen? Bill screwed up. Why did Bill screw up? Because we didn't train him. Why didn't we train him? Because there wasn't a budget for training. Why wasn't there a budget? And on and on. *Why* questions are useful for determining the root cause of problems, but are a dangerous backwater for gathering information. Use *what, where, when, who,* and *how* instead.

Ecology

One of the main reasons to use the meta-model is to help customers discover the possible drawbacks of any given approach to solving their problem. Prototypers, because of their experience, must help the customer see the technological quicksand and tar pits on the road to the solution.

If a technical solution will meet a customer's immediate needs, but hurt the company long term, it is the prototyper's job to bring the issue up and get it resolved. There are many things the prototyper must do behind the scenes to ensure the customer's system will have strong roots, stems, and leaves and be planted in fertile soil. These will be discussed in more detail in Chapter Five. It must be mentioned here because, as people integrate more software and hardware into their day-to-day existence, these systems must work together, serve each other, and support all who share in their activities. The program trading that caused the stock market collapse in 1987 is one example of technology missing an ecological component to protect everyone, not just the program traders.

There are several different ways to check that what the customer is asking for is ecologically sound:

1. Check for incongruence. Remember a time when someone agreed to something in a wishy-washy voice or with a bent posture or shaking head? That's incongruence and you'll need sensory acuity to notice it. Based on their response, you can respond, "It doesn't look/sound/feel like that's quite right. What haven't we discussed that would make this better?"

2. Ask the customer directly about the future, "Are you aware of any problems this might cause or do you have any personal objections to having this now?" Some other questions to ask are: Who else might this affect? What could go wrong? When might this be inappropriate? How could the system be made better to aid and protect everyone involved?

3. Ask the customer directly about the past, "What stopped you from doing this in the past?"

4. Ask the customer about similar problems, ''Where else have you experienced problems like this one?''

5. Exaggerate! Both positively and negatively, ''When we get this system up and running it will be the end of all of your worries. No more problems, ever!'' Or, ''This system will have terrible problems if you don't tell me where the pitfalls are. It will never work and I refuse to proceed until you tell me where the tar pits are.''

6. Use the customer's imagination to look forward in time: ''Imagine what it will be like a year from now when this new system is up and running. Notice what you will lose, both personally and professionally, and what can be done now to change the system to resolve those problems.''

7. Use the customer's imagination to look back from the future, ''Act *as if* you had already been using this new system and look back toward the present; notice how the system has worked, and what other changes are required to make it better.''

8. Use the customer's imagination to view the system from someone else's point of view: ''Who else might this affect? What problems would your supervisor/suppliers/customers have with this new system? How could the system be made better to serve and protect everyone involved?''

9. Have the customer ''role play'' the new environment: ''Pretend that this new system is working perfectly. How does it help or hinder you in the various aspects of your job? What's different? What works and what doesn't?''

I often ask at least some combination of these ecology questions because every system serves not only a short-term need, but must also fit into the long-range corporate strategy. Too many systems have been built that met the needs of one department at the expense of another, which causes waste, rework, turf battles, lower employee morale, and lower profits. Every system, whether it knows it or not, has a higher goal—a meta-outcome—that transcends the immediacy of the application being created.

Discovering Benefits

The meta-model helps the prototyper chunk down through the customer's confusion to reveal what they must have and want, specifically. To determine what each need will do for the customer, however, we need to chunk up a level or more to determine what that activity will do *for* them. In the Bell Labs reporting example mentioned earlier, for example, if the analyst had asked the meta-outcome question: ''What would that do for you?'' the customer would have responded, ''That would help eliminate the work I have to go through to revise these numbers when they're only slightly different from the previous report.'' Then the analyst could have asked the question again, ''If we could eliminate that rework, *what would that do for you?*'' ''That would free up three days a month that I spend revising those numbers so that our construction projects will stay focused.'' ''And if you could eliminate the rework and save those three days, *what would that do for you?*'' ''That would make me more productive, reduce errors, and ultimately mean that I could provide more value to the corporation and receive more recognition and reward in return!''

Notice how the meta-outcome question works to raise the issue up to a level where the outcome is much clearer than it was before. Now the analyst could say, ''What would happen if we could do all of that work for you?'' Now you've got an excited customer, because they know what's in it for them and so do you.

Organize the Information

Once the prototyper has begun to gather information about the requirements and the customer's meta-outcome, he or she must begin to organize the information into three categories: present situation, desired outcome, and new or existing resources required to achieve the customer's needs. The present state reflects how things are done now—the people involved, the process used, and the technology employed. The meta-model is extremely useful for gathering and sorting this information into useful categories. The essence of gathering this data is to create the backdrop against which we can create and compare the customer's future desired outcome.

Using the meta-model, we can further search the customer's communication for a description of what they desire in the future. In the previous section we looked at ways to tell the customers' needs from wants and wishes. Needs are expressed by words such as *must, should, shouldn't, have to,* and *can't.* These modal operators of *necessity* and *impossibility* direct the prototyper to the elements that simply must be in the initial prototype and avenues to exceed customer expectations by overcoming previously impossible barriers.

The modal operators of *possibility*, such as *want, could, would,* and *wish,* identify the elements of the system that will make the system more valuable over time, but are not essential to the initial creation process. These items should be entered into a change management system for future evaluation and implementation using the evolution process.

Next, the prototyper identifies the resources, such as people, processes, and technologies, that are in place to support the existing system and those that will need to be added to achieve the customer's objectives.

This data gathering and organizing goes on before a single line of code or a prototyping workstation is touched. Adequate planning will ensure a focused prototyping effort that will succeed more easily and effortlessly than can be imagined. Once the planning has gathered sufficient information to know the essential elements of the system, the party can begin.

DO

I call it a party because once the customer's needs are well developed, the prototyping team can turn to the task of rapidly creating and evolving the prototype. Creating the prototype is a wildly exciting time of discovery and accomplishment. Creating the prototype requires both a process for prototyping and the technology to support it. The prototyping process is described in Chapter 5.

Given the customer's needs and the prototyping process, the prototyper is now in a position to turn, at last, to appropriate technology for implementation. Until now, it is unlikely that a prototyper could know exactly what kind of hardware and software combination will be required to implement the customer's desires. There are personal computers, workstations, database machines, minicomputers, mainframes, and supercomputers. Any one or multiples may be chosen as an architecture for the future system. At this point, the only way a prototyper can go wrong is to implement the system on a platform that cannot be delivered. For example, if the prototyper creates the system on a personal computer using a database package, when it must ultimately run on a mainframe and support hundreds of users, the prototyper is in trouble. When customers see a working product that does what they want, they want it *now* not later!

CHECK

Once the prototype has been created, it is time to check its fit with the customer's expectations and evaluate how to make it better. This is also an excellent time to gather more information using the meta-model. When the customer says, "I don't like that," it's time to ask, "What don't you like about it, specifically? What could it do that would be better?" The response to these questions spawns the next round of changes as the prototyper acts to improve the system and elevate it to operational status.

One of the great things about a prototype is that the very word conveys a sense of incompleteness. This means that we don't expect everything to be perfect and that we do expect the original design to evolve dramatically over time. This helps the customer because they aren't on the spot to prespecify the requirements when they don't really know exactly what they want or what is possible.

Testing or checking the prototype leads to the fourth step of the PDCA process—taking action to continuously improve the prototype, the prototyping process, and the prototyper.

ACT TO IMPROVE

Once the prototyper has checked and compared the prototype with the customer, the time has come to *act to improve* the prototype *and* the customer's prototyping process and technology. Improving the prototype is a simple process of returning to step 1, rapport, and repeating the prototyping process. This, however, is not enough.

To become excellent at prototyping, or anything else for that matter, prototypers must act to improve the process they are using and their own personal skills. Improving the process consists of evaluating what went wrong and transforming these learnings into a means of improving the prototyping process to prevent those problems in the future. This process of continuous quality improvement will be discussed in Chapter 10. To improve their skills, prototypers must use a mental skill called "tape editing."

Tape editing is a technique for changing what we've learned and reinstalling better patterns. To begin, find a quiet place, close your eyes and drift back to your experience with the customer or the process or the technology. As you watch the movie of this experience, notice what you did well and what you could have done better. Then, like a Hollywood producer, cut out the parts that you could have done better, and insert a new strip of film in which you can see yourself doing this activity as perfectly as possible. When you're done editing, run the movie from start to finish and then simply store it away.

Tape editing creates a much more powerful learning experience than if you simply left the old movies as they actually occurred. And just think about how you could use this process with your loved ones or your favorite sport. What would happen if you instinctively used this advanced technology to improve your personal life? Would it have any impact on your professional career?

Well now we've talked about the people aspects of prototyping—from developing rapport to tape editing your abilities. We've discussed the process for gathering and organizing the information to create the prototype. In addition, we've looked at how to test the requirements with your customer and then act to improve the product, the prototyping process, and your skills. Now let's look at a few common problems during the requirements gathering process.

REQUIREMENTS DEFINITION PROBLEMS

"The Nibble"

In software requirements, customers often use an old negotiating ploy called "the nibble." The nibble comes after the contract is signed and the handshakes are done. The customer comes back and says, "Oh, by the way, I forgot this one small thing. Do you think you can squeeze it in?" Most prototypers will agree to include the change, but then the customer has you. Nibble follows nibble until it's all your fault that the system hasn't been delivered on time and on schedule. Just try to tell your customer at the eleventh hour how much their nibbles have cost and how much you need to delay the schedule. They will be indignant and well they should be because you failed to manage their expectations along the way.

The best response to the nibble begins at the bargaining table with a response that says, "I'd be glad to. How much are you willing to add to the price and schedule?" In other words, nibble back. It's all fair in negotiation.

Wrong User

Many customers are not users. During requirements gathering, managers or representatives participate, not the real users of the system. This will give you a clear map of what a manager thinks the system *should* do, but not what it needs to do to work in the real world with real users. To overcome this problem, include real users not their supervisors or some other intermediary. Include users that span the whole system from input to out-put, from programmers to operations, from managers to craft. Otherwise you will only get part of the total picture and the parts you get will be skewed.

Tom Sawyer

Prototypers are sometimes tempted to lay off their work on customers and vice versa. Don't whitewash any fences that aren't yours and don't expect the customer to tell you how to design the system to meet their needs. You're the expert in information technology, not them. Lead them! Offer options. Give them choice. They will love you for it.

The Way We've Always Done It

New systems or replacements for existing systems meet with resistance to change. You can anticipate these problems and create bridges from where the customer is to where they want to be. An ounce of prevention is worth a pound of cure. Identify ways to minimize the ''psychological cost'' of changing to the new system.

Inflexibility

An inflexible prototyper is an unhappy prototyper. Keep an open mind and leave the door open to continuous change in requirements until the prototype is complete.

Ignorance Is Bliss

Living in the world of technology is fine, but if you really want to learn the language, go live among the natives. Move into the customers' area and learn their job. Do it for a day or two. They're used to the process; you're not. By doing their job for a few days, you'll see new ways to simplify and streamline their whole operation in the new system.

Leaping into the Future

Technicians have a tendency to leap into the latest new technology as a way to learn it while delivering customers the latest in the state of the art. Unfortunately, this can backfire because of cost, time constraints, and so on. To overcome this problem, use the technology you're most familiar with to maximize productivity and then ease into new technologies on your time, not theirs.

Staying in the Past

Clinging to the old ways is as dangerous as leaping too far into the future. Have training lead improvements in technology and then blend it into the prototyping process. Feel free to let go of the old technologies and methodologies when they are no longer useful. Seek to understand and get a handle on new ways before going "whole hog" into new technologies.

SUMMARY

Various ways to begin building a relationship between the prototyping team and the customer have been presented in this chapter. The critical factor in successful requirements definition begins with establishing and expanding rapport with the customer. Once we trust each other, the prototyping team can begin to gather and organize the customer's requirements into the present situation, the desired situation, and essential resources required to achieve the desired outcome. By using the meta-model, the prototyping team can clarify the customer's requirements to any specific level of detail. During this information gathering process, the prototyping team can use the meta-outcome question to determine the customer's ultimate requirements.

From the richness of their descriptions, the prototyping team can identify the customer's needs, wants, and wishes. They can also identify possible problems in the overall system ecology and they can identify potential opportunities that might have otherwise been overlooked.

Requirements is an ongoing process of working with the customer to ensure that we create the key components of the system correctly during the initial development. From there on, these requirement gathering tools can be put into service to aid the evolutionary processes that follow.

Now that we have ways to successfully gather the user's needs, we can look at the actual prototyping process to turn dreams into technology. Walt Disney called it "imagineering."

CHAPTER 5

Rapid Prototyping

The rapid prototyping method of development is contrary to our standard method of developing systems. There was a problem getting technical people to work that way. They had a concern that they were generating a poor quality system.

— Boeing project manager (Rockart & DeLong 1988)

Different cultures view things differently: Americans and Europeans have a distinct past, present, and future; Hopi Indians have no words for any time except the present; and Arabs can see no further than a week or two into the future. This puts Americans in the unique category of those able to plan for the future, but compared to most Orientals, Americans are primitive. In America, the focus is on this quarter's profits and ''What have you done for me lately?'' In many Oriental cultures, future time spans hundreds of years. The Chinese leased Hong Kong to the British for 99 years, and now they are about to get it back. In Japan, for another example, mortgages may span three generations—father, son, and grandson. Rapid prototyping is sometimes viewed as yet another American desire to reap a crop almost as soon as the seed is sown.

For those of you who are paralyzed by the thought of doing things wrong, prototyping will kill you. Indecision is usually the worst mistake you can make. Prototyping, by design, ferrets out the fatal flaw and drags it out in the open for all to see. Then and only then can you take the kind of action required to change direction and solve the user's dilemma from a different perspective.

An application purchased from a vendor is perhaps the best kind of prototype. You can install it today and see how it works. After all, if the application is so well known that a vendor can offer the product, then it must be fairly stable and you should just buy it from them. Payroll and accounting systems are well known and thoroughly explored. Why create your own?

Or if the system isn't commercially available, you can visit someone who already has a similar application operational and ask them: "What works well and what doesn't?" If no such application exists and knowledge of the application is hazy at best, then you will need to fall back on rapid prototyping to develop an answer.

Rapid prototyping is the starting point of rapid evolutionary development (Figure 5.1). Rather than a minor part of the development process as it is in the requirements specification portion of a more traditional "construction" development process, prototyping plays a vital role in both the creation and evolution of software. Rapid prototyping, when done well, can reduce risk, enhance customer perceptions, and deliver more value in less time than any other method for software creation. Your customers, of course, will expect you to deliver whatever you show them. Satisfy their expectations and you will win a great victory. If you tell them that they will have to wait a couple of years for the "real" system to be delivered, you may lose the war.

Disposable prototypes have not worked. Creating a prototype simply for demonstration purposes is like gestating a baby for nine months and then, when the child is delivered, showing it to the mother briefly and then whisking it away forever. IS people then tell the customer that it's time to build a fully functional, adult system. Starting over again is not usually a well-received suggestion. The separation anxiety is so acute that customers scream and rave, and for good reason.

Fortunately, if you work together with the customer using the "right" tools in the "right" environment and with an eye on the vision of the future, you *can* use prototyping to create and deliver useful products quickly. Then you can grow and evolve the simple starting system into its future place in the business. If, however, you use the latest technical fad in an underpowered platform and ignore the ecology of the meta-system and the evolutionary path of the product, you are doomed to some of the worst technical and customer relations failures of your career.

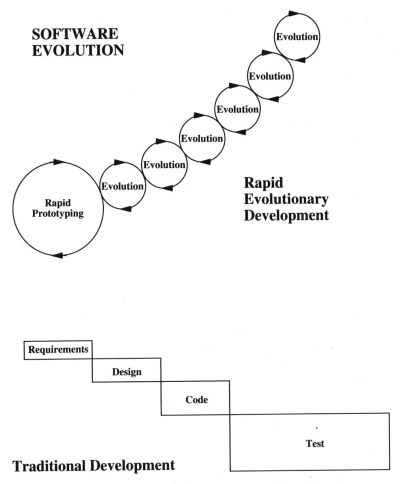

SOFTWARE EVOLUTION

Rapid Evolutionary Development

Traditional Development

Figure 5.1 Rapid Evolutionary Development vs Traditional Development

The school of data-driven prototyping . . . believes that prototypes should not be thrown away. Instead, they should evolve, extending the data architecture of the business in a process somewhat akin to learning.

— Dan Appleton (1983)

The best way to know what you want is to experience it first hand. Think about it: you experience cars, electronics, and numerous other products *before* you buy; why not software? Evolutionary prototypes help customers and prototypers get a hands-on feeling for the system as it develops.

This ongoing, experiential feedback allows us to learn from our mistakes and make continuous corrections as we move toward the customer's desired system.

Have you ever noticed that customers actually don't want systems; they want what the system will do for them—the benefits. If you think of a system as providing a service that will assist customers in achieving their goals and objectives, you will be that much closer to being able to meet their needs in a timely fashion.

INNOVATION

"The greatest pleasure in life is doing what people say you cannot do."
—Walter Bagehot (1826–77)

Innovation occurs when a small team of key people combined with resources, isolation, and esprit de corps do the seemingly undoable. This "skunkworks" approach changes the essence of how software is conceived and created. An evolutionary development team consists of top people, usually less than 25 percent of the normal team size. Prototypers share communication in many ways—sharing the same location, electronic mail, voice mail, and visual work areas all around. Prototyping projects also minimize paperwork.

Drucker (1986, pp. 134–139) describes the "do's" and "don'ts" of innovations. These rules sound surprisingly like the do's and don'ts of prototyping, because every prototype is an innovation.

Do's   1. Purposeful, systematic innovation begins with the analysis of opportunities.

Prototyping efforts begin by first looking for the right project to investigate. Doing a low value project quickly simply doesn't provide the returns required to support a prototyping effort.

2. Innovation is both conceptual and perceptual, therefore go out to look, to ask, to listen. "What does this innovation have to reflect so that the people who have to use it will *want* to use it, and see in it *their* opportunity?"

Prototyping begins by helping the customer establish a clear objective. The meta-model (see Chapter 3) is an essential tool for gathering the information required to understand the needs. The meta-outcome question (What will this do for you?) helps ensure that the customers will understand that the new system is their opportunity and will begin to develop their desire to use the system.

3. An innovation, to be effective, has to be simple and it has to be focused.

    Prototyping focuses on the vital 20 percent of the system that will provide 80 percent of the benefit. Anything else is excess weight that can bog a project down without providing commensurate value. Prototypes must focus strictly on the customers' needs, not their wants or wishes—only the vital 20 percent.

4. Effective innovations start small. Innovations had better be capable of being started small, requiring at first little money, few people, and only a small and limited market. Otherwise, there isn't enough time to make the adjustments and changes that are almost always needed for an innovation to succeed.

    Prototyping projects are explorations. They move most quickly when they have few people and a budget that may seem large for the explorer team, but small in comparison to other ventures.

5. A successful innovation aims at leadership.

    A prototype should aim at becoming the best it can be, given the boundaries of technology. It should exceed the customer's expectations and promise even more in their future.

Don'ts
1. Simply try not to be clever. Innovations have to be handled by ordinary human beings. Anything too clever, whether in design or execution, is almost bound to fail.

    Choose the simple over the complex; complexity will arrive on its own. If a prototype is too clever, the customer won't be able to use it and no one will be able to maintain or evolve it to meet business needs. Making a system complex is easy. Making the system simple, however, is often a difficult task.

2. Don't diversify, don't splinter, don't try to do too many things at once.

    Focus and create the user interface or data or processing

or interfaces to other systems. Don't try to do them all at one time. Do one thing at a time and do that one thing well.

3. Don't try to innovate for the future. Innovate for the present! Prototypers fail by trying to do everything the first time through the prototyping process. Prototype the vital 20 percent of the system for the present and leave the rest to the evolutionary process. This is not to say that the prototyper shouldn't keep the evolutionary future of the company in mind and do the ecologically correct things to ensure the quality and reliability of the system. Cutting corners in the creation process is a sure way to pay an even higher price in the evolution and survival of the system later on.

4. To Drucker's list, let's add: Don't avoid bad news, especially in the early stages of the prototyping process. During the prototyping process is the least expensive time to abort the project, especially if it shows signs of having genetic defects or putting an exhorbitant load on the parents.

Prototyping is a great way to converge on an innovative solution, but it can also be a way to go wrong in a hurry. The primary key to the success of the prototyping mission is the team assembled to do the work.

SUCCESSFUL PROTOTYPING TEAMS

The success of a prototyping team depends more on the teams than the methodology or technology used. The prototyping team is really a highly trained, but small force. Typically, there should be no more than 7±2 members on the team, including customer and users of the future system.

When a prototyping team finishes developing the initial working system, they should stay with it. Prototyping is an exhausting process. Like God at the end of six days of the Earth's creation, prototypers need some time off to rest before resuming the march toward the customer's ultimate objective. Shifting these people onto another arduous prototyping project would be foolhardy and not very ecological for the staff. Also, other members of your staff will want a chance to dig into the rapid evolutionary development process and achieve high goals. Let them, even use it as a reward for work well done.

The most successful prototyping teams have the following characteristics: they are small, dedicated, and responsive; the team members bring together the right mix of skills; they all have the personal skills to work well with customers; they have a good working knowledge of the software application; and they work in an environment separate from the rest of the company.

1. A small, flexible, independent, and responsive team, like the small entrepreneurial companies they emulate, can avoid the bureaucracy that so often infiltrates and paralyzes a larger unit. The skunkworks team must, however, be of an adequate size to complete the project. The right size will be 7±2 people (technical and customer) in the main team which can then drive several other similar sized groups of programmers if the project is large enough. No team should exceed 50 people total ($\sim 7^2$).

   If you doubt the value and capabilities of such smaller teams, consider the following: in 1953–1973, small U.S. firms (1,000 employees or fewer) produced 24 times more major innovations than did large firms (over 10,000 employees) and 4 times more than medium-sized firms (McEachron and Javitz 1987).

   Another example involves an early Cray computer. In 1965, Seymour Cray produced the CDC 6600 (Bell 1989). Thomas J. Watson, Jr., president of IBM Corp., wrote in a memorandum to his staff: ''Contrasting this modest effort with 34 people including the janitor with our vast development activities, I fail to understand why we have lost our industry leadership position by letting someone else offer the world's most powerful computer.'' Cray's retort was: ''It seems Mr. Watson has answered his own question.''

2. The right mix of skills—user interface, data, processing, interface, hardware, documentation, and training. From the beginning, prototyping teams must include customers, software professionals, vendors, and other key resources. Every prototyping team needs at least one wizard in each of these areas. Powerful user interfaces can no longer be designed by amateurs. Getting the data right is a significant challenge and the key to the evolutionary capability of the system. Interfaces to other systems must exist. No system is an island. Documentation is *software* for the human biocomputer that will use the system. No computing system is more complex. People often think that because they learned how to write in long hand in second grade that writing is a simple task that can be done by unskilled workers.

Most programming languages, for example, have only 50–150 verbs or commands. The data names are also restricted. The vocabulary of a computer is fairly small. Compare this to the 300,000 words in the English language and the 20,000 words that any high school graduate has at his or her command. Documentation is the software and training is the way the software is installed in a user's mind.

Prototyping teams are selected from the cream of available technicians. These individuals are often selected for their application knowledge and ability to work as a team in addition to their technical skills. Their knowledge of the business was at least as important as their technical expertise.

At the 9th International Conference on Software Engineering (IEEE 1987), Bill Curtis identified various members of a rapid development team:

- *Conceptualizer.* Keeper of the holy vision who understands the technology and application domains and integrates them
- *Boundary Spanner.* Mediates among members and other projects
- *Diagnostician.* Problem finder who knows the system structure
- *Technology Gatekeeper.* Champion of new technology
- *Feature Manager.* Maintains the integrity of application features
- *Generalizer.* Reusable component finder
- *Issue Manager.* Decision management and resolution
- *Usability Czar.* Maintains the usability of the system; this person believes that user needs, not designer fantasies, guide interface development

3. Personal skills are an essential part of establishing and maintaining rapport with the customer throughout the prototyping process. Each of the team members must have medium- to high-level skills in these areas. Chapter 3 described ways to establish and maintain rapport over time.

4. Knowledge of the application. Without an understanding of the application, the prototyper will fumble with the client's requests. The prototyper will need to learn the client department's functions to be able to create the system. This is slow. A knowledgeable prototyper can accellerate the process significantly.

5. A separate work environment. To succeed at their mission, the prototyping team must find a refuge from the rest of the company. If they don't, they will continually be hounded by their former boss for help; they will be pulled off the task by their friends. In other

words, there will be too many distractions. If you want your teams to really cook, find them a place where they can hole up with their customer and get into the frenzied mindset necessary for software creation. Skunkwork environments cement team loyalty and encourage rapid development.

Physical location plays a key role in success. Isolating the skunkworks staff in another building helps cut the bonds of past jobs and enable the prototyping personnel to get down to business. Isolated locations also help create the "special project" feeling that encourages people to stretch beyond their natural limits. If possible colocate the prototyping team with the hardware platform used. This gives the prototyping team hands-on control of all aspects of the system.

The physical layout of the prototyping environment is very important as well. The teams need many work rooms for impromptu meetings during the initiation and completion stage of the project. Then they need private offices to establish the flow necessary to produce results. To deliver this vital work time, allow project members to work at home or provide private offices to enable their success. This correlates with DeMarco and Lister's study (1985) that indicated that the top quartile of performers had enclosed offices.

Conference rooms need terminals and speaker phones to enable problem solving. Cover every spare wall with marker boards or electronic marker boards for concept sharing and development. Dedicate at least one wall to the overall system design.

Ensure plenty of light and ventilation throughout the space. Restrooms should be easily accessible. Supply coffee machines and refrigerators and microwaves to encourage the staff to stay close to the work. In general, do anything you can to support the needs of the staff. A good copying machine and a facsimile machine are also required.

The prototyping team can and should be isolated from the rest of the company. This protects and nurtures the team during its incubation period.

Forming the right team and giving it the right environment will help establish the essential requirements for successful prototyping efforts. Once a team is formed, it must begin evaluating the customer's needs. To succeed the team needs to focus on a small subset of the entire functionality. People have only a limited ability to reason about complex systems and their use. A successful prototyping effort must:

1. Start with a specific business need, preferably a high priority one.

(Caution: do not attempt a high priority prototyping project until you have a few medium priority successes under your belt.)

2. Identify and prioritize the customer's overall information needs, focusing on the 20 percent that will give 80 percent of the return on investment. There is never enough time to do everything, so don't try. Instead focus on the important rather than the critical, value rather than bells and whistles. Strive for explicit goals and scope.

3. Use the information gathering process described in Chapter 4 to elicit the customer's specific requirements for this 20 percent, capturing any additional requirements for future evolutions of the system.

4. Work rapidly to accommodate the user's changing understanding of their needs. Prototyping is a learning process, not a frozen one.

5. Manage the customer's expectations of the prototyping effort. Before you begin, educate the customer in exactly what you intend to do: Create the 20 percent and then grow the other 80 percent using successive evolutionary releases. Creation and evolution are as different as pregnancy and child rearing. Let your customer know in advance what to expect.

6. Ensure adequate resources to support the effort. Prototyping eats people, machines, and money. Planned parenthood always beats unplanned parenthood.

The software developers should be skilled in the tools of their trade—design, documentation, code, database, and testing tools. Given the tight development schedule for prototyping projects, it would be impossible to train everyone in the methodology and cockpit to be used and then to expect them to deliver.

The team should take time at the beginning to develop a strong working relationship. This provides two key benefits: trust and a common understanding that facilitates communications during the project. This is a useful time to draft a project plan that will be one's key to success.

Once the team has formed and begun to create a project plan, specialists will begin to take responsibility for portions of the project. Some will assume control of the system architecture. In small groups, others will begin to focus on each of the various application parts. This follows Alan Kay's philosophy that "the most productive team is two people in a room." This also reflects the views of Arno Penzias, Vice President, Bell Labs: "I manage a thousand people, but the work gets done in twos and threes."

7. Identify champions to adopt the initial system and participate in its evolution. People who believe in the system and what it can do will *make it work*. They will find avenues that others thought were impossible. Where other people would throw up their hands in disgust, champions will *find a way*. Champions work miracles.

8. Establish and ensure frequent deliverables and checkpoints to gain commitment and buy-in. That is, get out of the gate and start demonstrating functionality as quickly as you can. This will increase the feedback you receive and expand the relationship you're developing with the customer. Absence does *not* make the heart grow fonder.

Pitfalls of Prototyping

Regardless of how well you attempt to provide these simple criteria, you will still run into various tar pits on your way to prototyping success:

1. Fail to manage the expectations of customers and the excitement of the prototyping team. Unmet expectations lead to frustration, loss of motivation, and a loss of momentum that can be devastating.

2. Choose undersized or underpowered hardware and software platforms. Prototypers are often infatuated with something available on a personal computer that simply won't scale up to meet a customer's larger need. Prototypers also err by developing in a language that can't be delivered.

3. Fall into the "give them everything they ask for" trap that increases complexity and the risk of failure. Prototypers must be masters of the word *no* and project managers must help them maintain their focus.

4. Antagonize the people who control the information required to create the system.

5. Omit key players or involve too many in the new system. Evolution is the growth of the application's abilities to suit a particular customer. Systems expand rather than grow through the inclusion of an increasing number of people. Try to satisfy everyone and you will satisfy no one.

6. Focus on one aspect of the system to the exclusion of the others.

Creating the user interface, functionality, or performance will cause a considerable expense to fit the result to the rest of the system.

THE PROCESS

Returning to the Genesis model of software development—creation and evolution—God created our earthship in six (7 – 1) days according to Christian beliefs. Similarly, the genesis of most prototypes is an intensive period of creation followed by a never ending series of periodic evolutions. The initial prototyping process is a vibrant period of prototypers and customers working together to create a little, test a little, and tune, tailor, and tweek the system toward its initial incarnation. Every day during the prototyping process consists of many miniature software development life cycles—plan, do, test, and act to improve. Prototypers make user needs operational as quickly as possible to generate feedback that allows growth and evolution to occur at a phenomenal pace.

There are several types of prototyping processes:

- Exploration of various alternative approaches to verify feasibility
- Experimentation to clarify and verify requirements for development (an original model on which something is patterned) provides a demonstration prototype
  - Simulation of interfaces, functioning, and so on.
  - Closest to original meaning
  - Also a dead horse
- Growth and evolution to deliver a working product (first full scale and functional form of a new type or design)
  - Field and production prototype
  - Furthest from original meaning of the word prototype, but also most powerful.
- Incremental evolutionary steps to develop expanding versions of the system

Any of these approaches may focus their efforts on data or processing. Data-driven prototyping is better for business applications. Process-driven prototyping is better for real-time applications.

Data-Driven Prototyping

Data-driven prototyping uses an *abstraction* approach to development rather than a traditional, functional *decomposition* approach. Data-driven prototyping focuses on the data entities in a system from which all knowledge of the business derives. Entities transcend application boundaries for reuse by all who need them. Changes in the content, meaning and structure of data entities reflect the evolutionary, learning, growing, and maturing of all business processes.

Like the combined knowledge of cultures and libraries, or the genetic coding in DNA, data doesn't die when an application retires. It grows through interaction with the application and passes its information on to future generations of systems. Systems integration occurs to the extent that two applications share the same data.

Data prototypers seek to discover and create the integrating data in the most effective and efficient way. Traditional construction of systems has ignored this approach and only now are the effects becoming obvious. Data prototypers use prototyping to:

- Validate information requirements
- Discover the optimum structure for data
- Encourage bottom-up integration
- Define processes to compute or derive new information from derived data; this is the essence of abstraction
- Evaluate database efficiencies
- Improve physical database design
- Anticipate evolutionary changes and plan for them in such a way as to minimize their impacts
- Facilitate database implementation

The process of data-oriented prototyping is simple and straightforward, even if the activity surrounding it is not:

1. Conceptual data design (business entity modeling)
2. Physical data design and implementation through prototyping
3. Evaluation against existing and future requirements scenarios
4. Performance analysis and improvement

Application-Driven Prototyping

In most applications, the system holds the data hostage. This approach, applied to business systems, tends to create information pollution. Application-driven prototyping encourages every system to have its own internal version of the same information, none of which are totally correct or synchronized with all of the other systems that use the same data. Then when one system tries to feed data to another, there is a certain amount of toxicity that causes stomach upset in both the system and the people maintaining it.

Real-time systems, however, are much more *event* driven than *entity* driven. Application-driven prototyping is a valid approach to real-time systems.

Simple Prototyping Process

The Price of Success: "Dedication, hard work, and an unremitting devotion to the things you want to see happen."

A strong, but flexible methodology ensures the success of the project. The prototyping process follows the PDCA cycle of growth and evolution. A simple version of this methodology would be:

1. Gather a small, focused set of requirements
2. Evaluate alternatives and create a working model
3. Test for correctness with the user
4. Act to improve the set until both IS and the user are satisfied
5. Loop through steps 1–4 until sufficient functionality is available that the users are licking their chops in anticipation of using the system
6. Test to ensure that the system is industrial strength
7. Release the system to a pilot group
8. Loop through steps 1–7 until everyone is satisfied
9. Release the system for general use

Rigorous Prototyping Process

A more customized version of the rapid prototyping methodology consists of: project planning, functional requirements, evolutionary architecture, design, code, test, and installation and support.

Project Planning. Project managers create and adjust the original project plan draft using the only factors available—overtime and system content (the 20 percent that gives 80 percent of the value)—to meet the deadline. Most of the prototyping group may work long hours during the creation process. This is only possible for the initial, short development period. Additional effort at this level will result in illness and absenteeism. Plan on the staff taking a two week break following conversion and celebrate their success.

Most overtime can be avoided by anticipating the actual time it takes to get office space, select and install computer hardware and software, hire staff, and so on. In doing so, the project can start sooner and have more time to create additional functionality.

The project managers continue to adjust the scope and content of the system as the project progresses.

Since the system is an evolutionary prototype, prototypers need to establish a minimum acceptable level of software quality. This entails certain levels of standards to ensure consistency. These standards include:

- Design and development standards
- A list of approved abbreviations (data naming consistency)
- A data dictionary
- Skeleton design and coding specifications to enhance productivity
- Change control of all completed work products
- Test case development

Functional Requirements. The development team then begins gathering and documenting the initial functional requirements for the system. Walkthroughs and inspections of requirements are used to ensure their quality and accuracy.

Evolutionary Architecture. Prototyping team members then partition the functional requirements into functional areas and establish a flexible, evolutionary architecture for the initial development of the prototype. To allow smaller prototyping teams to work independently, establish interface standards that specify the flow control and integration of all functional areas. These standards improve productivity by simplifying integration and system testing.

Design. Because the prototyping team is using a more flexible, evolutonary process for system creation does not mean that they have to forget everything they know about existing methods of development. The prototypers can still use top-down, structured, modular design. Developers can reuse skeletal designs to specify the design. This approach assures the flexibility of the resulting system and the ability to react quickly to changes in user requirements.

Place particular emphasis on creating an excellent, evolutionary data design. This leads to creation of a system that can grow with the company. Otherwise, you will create the same old garbage, only faster.

Code. During the coding process, prototypers can use the most powerful language available to create the core system. Prototypers will find creating the core application relatively easy, while writing the interfaces and conversion routines to existing systems will take most of the time and effort.

As with designs, the prototyping team will inspect the code to ensure quality.

Test. Rapid evolutionary development testing consists of the standard unit, integration, and system and acceptance testing. Test plans and test cases grow as the system grows. Because of the interface standards, the product will be easier to test. Customer interfaces can be tested almost immediately. Unit testing of the various subsystems follows.

System test cases are prepared as the system evolves to facilitate testing. Test results are inspected to ensure quality.

Installation and Support. The prototyping team prepares the end-user training material in parallel with the development effort. Users, in order to prepare for the system's delivery, can administer this course using an older prototype with some missing functionality.

You may find it useful to have a mission control room for the conversion and installation.

Change Management. Because the prototypers know that changes are inevitable, they can choose to manage change throughout the creation and evolution of the system. A change management system is essential to support this effort. All changes and problem reports are then tracked through the following steps:

1. Requirements changes
2. Function design changes

3. Evolutionary architecture changes

4. Code modification

5. Testing

6. Release

On-Line Systems

To develop an on-line system,

1. Focus your energy in three main areas to begin with:
   a. Data models to begin creating the databases for the system as a stable, reusable platform for development of the system processing.
   b. On-line screens and reports to begin developing the look and feel of the system from the user's point of view.
   c. Transactions required to accomplish the system's objectives (e.g., calculations, add customer, update tax table). Model the simple transactions first and then the more complex ones.

2. Once these are somewhat stable, you can begin creating the processing required to:
   a. Access and update the databases (using information hiding principles).
   b. Transform the user's inputs into stored data and useful outputs.

3. Continue to grow the system to a working level that would provide at least 50 percent of the functionality required.

4. Put the system into a pilot location to work the remaining bugs out while continuing to evolve the system toward excellence. Remember: There is no failure, only feedback. Add only user *needs* to the system at this point, keeping the overall ecology of the system in mind. It has to be able to grow from this infant stage into adulthood, that is, minimize birth defects in the system.

5. Deploy the system across its user base and begin the evolution of the system toward its desired capabilities. Use the evolutionary process to schedule important enhancements to the system and keep ecology and evolutionary ability continuously in the forefront of everyone's mind. You can continue to apply rapid prototyping to the creation of major system enhancements as well.

Ecology Issues

For an evolutionary prototype to survive in the real world, it will need to take into account the ecology of the entire meta-system it enters. Living systems focus energy on maintaining ecology through:

- Minimizing impacts on existing systems and cultures
- Providing adequate documentation and training
- Ensuring quality: maintainability, flexibility, reusability, portability, reliability, and efficiency
- Focusing on needs versus wants or wishes
- Ensuring security
- Ensuring performance and response time of the delivered system
- Evaluating and providing evolutionary hardware requirements
- Minimizing cost
- Maximizing error handling and recovery (immune system response)
- Allowing backup and recovery
- Providing adequate resources for the task

If a developing prototype changes too fast without regard for ecology, no one can keep abreast of the changes or manage to synchronize all of the documents and deliverables. It can become impossible to test the system adequately in such tumultuous times. It will take time for the system to become self-sustaining. Prototypers must keep their thoughts on the system's future, not only its present. Toward this end:

1. No poorly structured design should be accepted
2. Any change that causes design deterioration must invoke a redesign of the affected system parts
3. Code that becomes obsolete through evolution must be replaced, not patched

Rapid prototyping gives you the time that "construction" takes away. In rapid prototyping, you always have time to make the system right *before* you release it, but you will never have time to do it over. You must keep ecology in mind.

TOOLS

During World War II, huge formations of bombers would gather to assault specific targets. It often took them hours to form the force that would attack a target and many times entire groups would miss the rendezvous. In today's world, a small, highly trained, heavily armed force flying the latest in advanced technology can strike with lightning speed against targets of opportunity as they are identified.

The old construction model of software development mirrors the World War II bombing raids. Rapid evolutionary development teams mirror the aerial strike forces of today.

The lure of the quick fix encourages us to buy a software tool and do what feels good, to do what is tension relieving instead of goal achieving. To succeed at rapid prototyping and to create an evolutionary prototype that can withstand the test of time, we must begin with the languages and environments where the system will live. If the system will live in a COBOL, mainframe environment, by all means create the prototype in COBOL on the mainframe. If the system will live in a C or C++ world on a Unix box, then create it there. If you have to go through two or three different types of environments to determine which is the best, then by all means do so.

For example, I wrote my first software metrics analyzer in COBOL in 1979. It didn't work fabulously, but I learned so much from doing it, that it was easier to do the next one in Unix Shell, and the next one in awk, and the final versions in the Unix lexical analyzer. Each successive tool and environment took less time because I more thoroughly understood the application. I'm sure that if I had tried to learn the application and the lexical analyzer all at one time I would have given up. As it was though, it only took me eight months to go from the COBOL version to the complete suite of lexical analyzers I created for COBOL, PL/I, and C.

Most people tend to look for something tangible—new technology—as the key to a project's success, but they often overlook the other obvious success factors. In the case of rapid evolutionary develement, technology plays an important, but not a critical part. People and processes play an even greater role in achieving software success.

Software Issues

A major factor in prototyping software selection should be its speed, flexibility, and familiarity among the prototyping team. There are four key technological components that must be created for any software system:

1. The user interface: input, output, and query
2. Data: bases, tables, files, and so on
3. Processing: algorithms, computations, and so on
4. Interfaces to other systems

Hardware Issues

Hardware technology is accelerating at remarkable rates. Power is moving toward the customer in the form of personal computers and workstations, while minicomputers, mainframes, and supercomputers continue to expand their capabilities at a rate that doubles every two or three years. Systems that seemed impossible are now feasible and desirable.

Software development environments can now take advantage of many kinds of platforms and technologies to become massively more productive and effective. The Japanese Sigma project gives each engineer his own workstation (Akima and Ooi 1989). These dedicated 32-bit machines have powerful networking functions, resource-sharing functions, and advanced user interfaces—high-resolution display, mouse, and graphics support. User interfaces, especially for prototypers, must offer integrated text and graphics capabilities. Sound and color also assist the creation process.

Open Architectures

[The personal computer is like] an old testament God, with lots of rules, and no mercy.

— Joseph Campbell

Several different alternatives exist for prototyping platforms: desktop computers or desktop workstations connected to one or more larger computers. Prototypers are only as efficient as the environment they use. Open hardware and software architectures allow the maximum flexibility for changes in functionality and technology. Closed architectures tend to trap prototyping teams in technological quicksand. Proprietary technology is its own tar pit.

From this perspective, an operating system such as Unix which runs on a wide variety of platforms is a strategic weapon. Unix offers portability and flexibility that you will be hard pressed to find elsewhere. It has several strategic advantages:

1. It frees you from dependence on a single hardware vendor

2. It runs on a broad range of computer architectures, from personal computers to supercomputers
3. It comes with loads of reusable components
4. It is the user interface of the future (workstations all run Unix)
5. Expert systems and parallel processing environments rely on Unix
6. The tools you've grown to love in MS-DOS are migrating to Unix

Unix runs on more types of computers than any other operating system (Cureton 1988). It offers windowing (X Windows among others), relational and semantic databases, extensive networking and communication, and expert systems. Sun, Digital, IBM, Apollo, and HP all have some form of Unix workstation.

Virtually all vendors are working toward a true integrated project support environment (IPSE), a software cockpit where prototypers can grow and evolve software with ease. Visions of a software cockpit grew out of the dynamic changes that have rocked the software industry. Most companies have a large suite of relatively independent applications that were both internally and externally developed. It has, however, become essential to realign and integrate our information systems to meet the competitive challenges of the 1990s.

Based on the three key elements of an effective software cockpit— people (the pilots), process (how to fly a software mission), and tools (the plane)—the analogy between pilots and software professionals is so apt that the "software cockpit" can serve as the overriding vision of how people will create software in the future.

Vision

During World War II, the outcome of the war was largely decided by control of the air. In the latter stages of the war, huge constellations of bombers and fighters pounded the Axis. In today's combat environment (we call it competition), a few high-tech aircraft with advanced weaponry can perform these feats.The battleground of the 1990s will be information. To meet the challenges of the information economy, the massive software efforts of the past must give way to smaller, faster, more versatile groups of highly trained software pilots working in advanced software environments.

The analogy can be extended further to describe software projects as one of the following:

General aviation	End-user computing (EUC)
Commercial aviation	IS software creation and evolution
Military aviation	Offensive and defensive product deployment
Space exploration	New market development

Each of these analogies can benefit from rapid evolutionary development. To develop the software cockpit of the future, the hardware and software tools and methods must be chosen to reflect the type of mission a software pilot performs. For example, the personal computer of an end-user may be completely inappropriate for a quick strike into an information technology market and vice versa.

Yet, like aircraft pilots, software pilots will share certain common needs and abilities. For example, all three of these missions—EUC, IS, and product—require a plan for completion—a flight plan. Some of the requirements that software pilots might share are:

- Project management (flight planning)
- Flexible methodology to match the type of software mission
- Instrumentation: measurement of progress, direction, altitude, and so on
- Advanced human factors interfaces: heads up displays, sound, video

These skills can be likened to ground school (programmer basic training) and flight school (evolutionary training). They teach a software pilot to fly, but only the basic skills needed for general aviation. To become a commercial or military software pilot, we will need additional rigor, discipline, and training to handle the specifics of each type of mission. A strong training program helps eliminate the cultural shock of change.

This evolutionary environment is a conceptual view of the software cockpit for development and evolution. It exists independent of methods, tools, and hardware platforms. It incorporates the critical success factors of people, process (how work is done), and technology (to support the process).

The Cockpit

Personal computer development environments offer enough power to handle end-user computing problems, but not nearly enough to handle the needs of IS or offensive software creation and evolution. Engineering

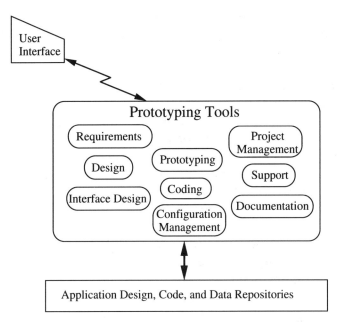

Figure 5.2 Rapid Evolutionary Development Environment

workstations (cockpits) coupled to a dynamic repository (mission control) seemed the best route to follow (Figure 5.2). Most available vendor products, however, offer one of two things: only a small part of the cockpit or a closed architecture that would prohibit integration and choice.

Since vendors have no incentive to achieve integration and openness, you might as well do the best you can with the available packages that are both open and extensible.

Cockpit Overview. If you want an open architecture, about the only way you can get it from more than one vendor is through Unix. Only through its multitasking and integration capabilities can you create the environment desired. Unix workstations offer an excellent hardware platform for the software cockpit. The Japanese reusability project—SIGMA—has moved in this direction, using a Unixlike variant.

To simplify creation and evolution, the cockpit will need a repository of data, designs, code, and other reusable components that can be shared by all the pilots.

You can't create the supersoftware cockpit of the future until, like aviation of the past, you have some sort of an initial dashboard that can then evolve to fully meet your needs. The SEI maturity framework described in

Chapter 1 will cause rapid shifts in methods and tools if you move rapidly toward excellence. The cockpit needs the flexibility to change and grow with the software process.

Process Specifics. Many companies have found that in the race to automate the software process, tools can lock you into an ineffective process. These tools are ultimately abandoned because they don't help people get the job done. Deming (1986) suggests that any process (including software) that is not under some form of quality management wastes 25–40 percent of all effort and expenditures. Looking at the "debugging industry" that threatens all software projects, either creation or evolution, you have to address not only the technological aspects of cockpit, but the process issues as well. Before you can automate the process, you must define and streamline the software process. Florida Power and Light, winner of the 1989 Deming Prize, found that methodology was more important than tools for improving productivity and quality in their IS department. Projects are not all alike. So one process or methodology cannot encompass the full range of software missions, just as no one flight plan, airplane, or pilot can perform all aviation missions. There are, however, some common activities that must be addressed, but the bulk of the methods used in any project should be modular and flexible and fit into this backbone process. This leads us to the concept of a flexible, evolutionary methodology that supports a wide variety of methods that can be selectively chosen for a given project.

Flexible Methodology. The methodology assumes that there must be some planning, doing, checking, and acting to improve in any project. It also assumes that we must manage quality, the project, system changes, and software configurations throughout the entire life cycle of a given project. Given the methods for each step, a team selectively chooses a method that matches their project and plugs it into the process. The methodology must be:

1. Simple
   a. Easy to understand
   b. Easy to learn and apply
2. General
   a. Cover all classes of projects
   b. Cover all kinds of people, process, and tools

3. Specific
   a. Provide useful situation specific advice

To accomplish these goals, the methodology needs a backbone that is both simple and general. The individual methods then accomplish each step.

Regardless of the project, a data-centered approach to creation and evolution is critical to creating new systems that are maintainable and flexible to meet our continued evolution. No matter how well a system is constructed, entropy will take its toll, like a jungle reclaiming a civilization in decline. To prevent this, you will need data, software, and documentation re-engineering tools.

Once the methods and tools are selected, pilots must be trained to fly the cockpit successfully.

Pilot Training. In traditional aviation education, pilots first study in "ground school" and then graduate to "flight school." A similar approach would work well for software pilots. The ground school for data- and growth-oriented pilots consists of three phases:

1. Data-focused creation
2. Object-oriented composition
3. Rapid evolutionary development

Learning to think "data first" is a tough concept. Everyone wants to leap over ground school and start flying software. There are more than enough burning hulks that suggest that this is not a prudent way to learn to fly.

Real pilots spend a significant amount of time in flight simulators experiencing all kinds of flight conditions—good and bad—before they climb into an aircraft. Software pilots, however, often take their first solo flight in bad weather in a project that is already behind schedule, overloaded, and poorly balanced. Training needs to offer software pilots a project flight simulator that takes them through the kinds of turbulence and problems that a project commonly experiences.

Finally, pilots will need flight school. As Brooks (1975) identified, adding people to a late software project makes it later. Because our best pilots spend most of their time teaching new people how to fly, projects seldom benefit from their expertise. Wouldn't it be better to send new people up in a mock project or a low risk one? A certified instructor or "copilot" could go along with them to show them things that they would otherwise learn the hard way. What we need is "Top Gun" for software pilots, especially those who will fly the highly competitive missions of rapid evolutionary development. This flight school will be an expensive but necessary step on the road toward highly productive creation of quality software.

Software Cockpit. Begin building your software cockpit on Unix workstations coupled with other host computers—Unix, IBM, and so forth. Choose platforms and tools that offer:

1. Open architecture—for flexible choice
2. Extensibility—to allow growth
3. Availability—to ensure reliability
4. Performance—to ensure productivity
5. Support of a defined process methodology

Choose your software pilot's basic instrumentation first. During a flight, for example, a pilot only uses five or six instruments to keep the aircraft aloft; choose a core of five to seven tools to aid the software pilot. Then, just as first generation aircraft contained very primitive tools, so too will the initial cockpit. The seven areas of concern are:

1. Project management
2. Quality management
3. Prototyping
4. Code generation
5. Documentation management
6. Change and configuration management
7. Release control

These seven items constitute the minumum set of tools for a successful mission. Other valuable tools include:

- A repository of data and reusable components
- Screen prototyping
- Report generation
- Measurement and analysis
- Query facilities

- Document creation (text, graphics)
- Fourth generation languages
- Relational database management systems
- Application generators

Because software is such an evolutionary medium, we should expect our tools to change and grow right along with our processes. Never become complacent. Budget time and money to upgrade your toolkit every year.

Testing

Tests cannot establish the absence of errors.

— *Edgar Dijkstra*

We can always run more tests, create more independent testing groups, inspect more designs and code, but if we are ever going to begin to run instead of walk, we must begin to improve our processes to prevent defects. A classic parable of this difference can be found in Guaspari (1985). (See Chapter 10 for more details.)

Most people use the Goldilocks Testing Method: Too few tests, too many tests, just the right number of tests to find the ''right'' problems instead of the ''wrong'' problems—problems the user would never experience. Increase your ability to find the right bugs by:

- Matching the test environment to the real environment
- Involving the user in testing the system
- Designing tests against historical faults and failures

Useful Techniques

There are other useful techniques that can assist in rapid prototyping. Storyboarding and parallel development are two such possibilities. We're all familiar with Walt Disney's animation wizardry, yet how many of us have thought to apply it to developing software? The cost of producing a short subject with 17,000 individually drawn and inked frames is high. The cost of producing a full-length movie with a quarter of a million images is immense. Disney Studios developed the technique of *storyboarding* to prototype the story line before they committed a single cartoonist to the first cell. Storyboarding uses small images posted on a board to show the logic, flow, and consistency of the evolving story.

Advertising firms use this technique to refine TV ads at a relatively low cost of $2,500 per storyboard compared to $100,000 to $200,000 per completed commercial. About two-thirds of all commercials are abandoned after storyboarding.

Storyboarding is also a useful technique during the conceptual stage of prototyping. It gets ideas up quickly where they can be evaluated, moved around, and kept or discarded. A "white" board and a flock of Post-it™ notes serve as the tools of choice. Write the names of players, tasks, data, objects, or whatever on the notes. Then put these up on the board and add, change, delete, or move them until a pleasing configuration appears.

Parallel development offers another possibility. Kick off two or more teams in the pursuit of a key strategic software goal. This will shorten the cycle and improve your chances of success. Since prototyping teams are small by comparision to traditional development teams, you can afford to splurge on two teams tackling the same problem. IBM used this approach for the personal computer. You can too.

Case Study

One large compiler development project (Hekmatpour 1987) found evolutionary prototyping of great benefit. The system was written primarily in Lisp and took 12 prototyping cycles and 2,613 staff hours of effort to converge on a solution. Figure 5.3 shows the growth and evolution of the prototype.

Lessons learned:

1. Use a disciplined approach
2. Use an open system architecture
3. Be selective in what you document and keep it up to date
4. Throw away bad code and rewrite it any time it will enhance the system's maintainability
5. Use available programming support environments
6. Keep the design clean and structured
7. Never optimize a prototype for efficiency during development; this can only introduce entropy into the system
8. Review products as they are developed and changed to ensure excellence

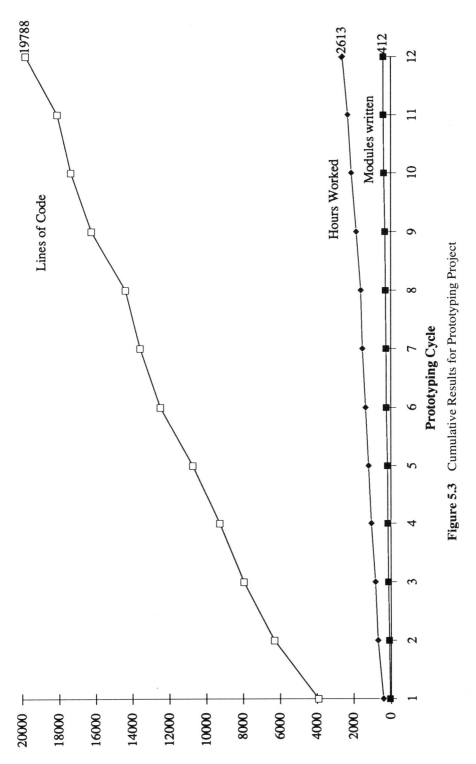

Figure 5.3 Cumulative Results for Prototyping Project

SUMMARY

The people and organization are the keys to the success of prototyping projects. These people then select the project management, creation, and evolution methods and tools that allow them to achieve the result required. The team chooses the technology required to support the rapid evolutionary development using these methods. Creating a team of customers and prototypers will produce the vital, initial 20 percent of the system's ultimate functionality in record time.

In spite of what might appear on the surface to be a chaotic development process, the prototypers follow a rigorous methodology that includes project management, quality control using inspections and testing, requirements specification, architecture and data design, detailed design, and code. High caliber prototyping staffs recognize the value of defined processes and standards. Together, prototyping team members can apply their cumulative experience to customize a streamlined methodology to match the project's objectives.

The use of rapid prototyping will result in a more usable and responsive system to meet the customer's needs. Evolution of the system will consume as much as 50 percent of the prototyping staff for problem solving and ''baby-sitting'' the existing system. To succeed at innovation and rapid evolutionary development, you must choose the right people, process, technology, and environment:

1. Build a small team with both the application and technical skills required to do the project in a quality way in the shortest period of time. Partition the project into smaller (1–3 person) work teams.
2. Use off-site training as a team-building experience. Create that ''special team'' esprit de corps.
3. Create a flexible project plan.
4. Let the team manage itself. For example, the team should be able to choose its own working hours and location.
5. Let the team select its physical environment (e.g., open work area, or enclosed offices with plenty of open area and conference rooms for communication), but isolate the people from their old work location.
6. Let the team choose its methodology and technology; let the team select and develop the standards they will use. People usually choose to do the job right using higher standards than you can possibly impose on them.

7. Put a chalk board on every blank wall.

8. Ensure the amenities are immediately available to support round-the-clock work (e.g., coffee machines, microwave, refrigerator).

9. Use inspections of all work products to assure quality of the delivered system. Testing alone cannot provide a quality product.

10. Use project management to track development activity and change management tools to track changes to requirements, designs, code, tests, and documentation.

11. Choose the development tools to match the development task. Different projects will require different tools.

12. Realize that any prototyping effort delivers only the first evolutionary system functionality. Prototyping delivers the key components of the system, but not the other 80 percent to make it fully operational. Many more evolutionary iterations will be required to create the ultimate product.

CHAPTER 6

Reuse

Why do schools teach almost nothing of the pattern which connects?
— *Gregory Bateson and Mary Catherine Bateson (1987)*

Using DNA, cells reproduce to create exact copies of themselves. Entire beings are created from a single initial cell. As the fetus grows, cells differentiate to form the various organs, tissues, muscles, nerves, and bones. To succeed at software reuse, we will need to follow a similar strategy.

The continuing success of rapid evolutionary development depends on the reuse of system parts and components—data especially, and then other components such as processing, documentation, and training. We must ask how is one thing related to another? What pattern connects them? One human is much like another, with two legs, two arms, a torso, and a head. Legs are much like arms, with five fingers and five toes and similar bone structures. Humans are also similar to horses and dolphins: We breathe air; we share limbs or fins, and a head with two eyes and a mouth. What are the similarities among software systems and how can we reuse them?

By emphasizing the creation and reuse of system components from current prototyping projects, a resource pool of data, software, and design documentation can begin to grow to meet the future needs of the corporation. Using these resources, prototypers can maximize their effectiveness and efficiency during the creation of new projects. This is especially important when working with third generation programming languages and tools.

There is an untapped potential for productivity gains through the reuse of standard software components.

— Ted G. Lewis and Paul W. Oman

It is often asked, "If reusability is so great, why haven't we already done it?" This is a good question and the answer is largely because reuse requires an investment. In a world of "get rich quick" schemes, reuse makes money the old-fashioned way: over the long haul. From Chapter 2, we can recall the basic laws of reuse:

1. Part of all you code is yours to keep
2. Start thy software repository to fattening
3. Make thy software multiply
4. Protect thy treasures from loss
5. Increase thy ability to develop reusable software

Another reason that we haven't made great strides in software reuse is that we lack the standards, parts, components, documentation, and retrieval tools that make reuse more viable. Unless threatened by competition, most companies won't ante the down payment to get started. The competition is there, however. Most companies just haven't seen it yet and by the time they do it will be too late. The Japanese, for example, have been forced to achieve high levels of reuse to maximize their productivity. Productivity for companies such as Hitachi and Fujitsu runs about 30,000 LOC per person year including reuse. Compared to recent American averages of 4,000–6,000 LOC per year, the reuse productivity rate is 5–7 times higher. MIT data (Gross 1991) shows U.S. productivity at 7,290 LOC per year and Japanese at 12,447 per year. In terms of defects, MIT data indicates that U.S. defect rates are 4.44/KLOC and Japanese are 1.96/KLOC. In other words, the Japanese are growing and reusing software twice as fast with half as many defects.

Japanese companies also help each other in ways that U.S. companies won't. Fujitsu, for example, introduced Kawasaki Steel to standardization and reuse in 1987; software productivity is now 2.5 times greater (Gross 1991). Reuse has another advantage: lower defect rates because of the robust testing each reusable component receives. Error rates in companies such as Fujitsu run at ten defects per million lines of code. The 1990 space shuttle software had 70 defects per million (i.e., about 35 in the flight software) and the American average is 3,000 defects per million. The only way to achieve low defect rates, high reliability, high productivity, and quality is to begin the creation of reusable system components.

At AT&T Bell Laboratories (Gruman 1988), two transaction processing projects of 120 KLOC and 210 KLOC achieved reuse rates of 65 percent. On one 1200 KLOC project, software reuse at the 86 percent level was achieved.

Software will form the competitive edge of companies in the next decade. IS departments must step off the slow productivity improvements of the last few decades (approximately 5 percent per year) and explore the new paradigm of software creation that will double or triple productivity in 3–5 years. Eric Sumner, AT&T Bell Labs' vice president for operations planning put it this way: "If there's a single key, it's reuse." Ted Biggerstaff (1989) says that improvements of 20–50 percent are reasonable *within a narrow application domain.* He also said that quality improves with reuse. "Quality comes along for free because you use the components that have been debugged and used extensively." Reuse offers prototypers a way to stop reinventing the wheel for common elements, parts, components and subsystems and to improve quality through rigorous testing of the reusable components. The incentives to reuse software parts in the creation of new systems are:

- Economic savings, especially for large complex projects
- Customer satisfaction through more reliable systems
- Prototyper satisfaction through faster creation of systems
- Prototyper stress reduction through focus on the creation of new components

Reuse changes the whole software process. The game becomes one of putting the puzzle together, not creating the pieces. This is a wonderful change because there's never a project that isn't under the gun.

REUSE PROCESS

The reuse process is actually very simple; doing it rigorously is what takes time and effort. In the reuse process, you will need to:

1. Identify reusable designs, parts, and components (Figure 6.1)
2. Create the reusable components

1. On-Line Processing
    • User Interface
        - Windowing
        - Screen Handling
        - Input, Query, and Output
        - Data Validation
    • Transaction Processing and Management
        - Transaction file creation for batch posting
        - On-line posting

2. Data Base (relational, semantic, hierarchical, network) or File Processing
    • Sorting, Merging, and Joining
    • Searching and Retrieving
    • Updating

3. Table Handling
    • Loading and Unloading
    • Sorting
    • Searching and Retrieving
    • Updating

4. Data Entry, Editing, and Validation

5. Batch Processing
    • Transaction Posting
        - Add, Change, and Delete
    • Query
    • File Maintenance

6. Reporting
    • Headings
    • Footers
    • Pagination
    • Control Breaks
    • Accumulating totals
    • Margin Control
    • Grouping lines on one page

7. Security and Integrity
    • Logon Authority
    • Data security - read, add, change, delete
    • Recovery and Restart

Figure 6.1   Reusable Parts and Components

3. Certify the quality of the reusable parts
4. Catalog and store the reusable parts for easy retrieval
5. Manage change to these reusable items

Identifying Reusable Parts

There is a simple test that will determine how easily you can grasp and use reusability techniques. Before you read the next paragraph, take a handful of coins out of your pocket and describe what you see.

There are two common and two more unusual responses to what people see. People who have the easiest time reusing software will notice first *how the coins are alike and then how they are different*. For example, some people will respond that they see American coins that are all round that have faces of former presidents on them. Others will see what they add up to: 72 cents or some such thing. These people first see how things are alike and then how they are different, which allows them to see how two functions are alike so that they could be reused. Then they see how the functions are different so that they know what will need to be uniquely created.

People who will have more difficulty reusing software will first notice how the coins are *different and then how they are similar*. For example, they will say: ''there's a penny, nickle, dime, and quarter. The penny is a copper color and they all have different obverse designs. They are all different sizes.'' These are all statements of difference. These people will then follow by saying how the coins are alike: ''they're all cents and round.'' A few people will be at the poles of this discussion: the coins will all be *exactly the same or completely different*. Any of these latter three types of people will have problems relating to reuse. To reuse software easily, you will need to first notice how things are alike and then how they are different. You learned this mental strategy early in life and it's easy to borrow and apply the optimal strategy to reuse once you know how your strategy is similar or different.

To initiate reuse, you must begin by defining the typical issues that arise when building some *class* of systems. Then you can begin to create reusable designs, code, and data from these generalizations. There are several types of reuse:

• Design, code, and data extraction and adaptation from other products
• Direct reuse from component repositories and databases

- Program generation
- Fourth generation language (4GL) usage

Design and code adaptation reflects that software engineering is often re-engineering, not art or invention. Adapting existing software requires clear documentation so that changes can be made safely. Adaptive reuse creates maintenance and configuration control problems (yet another component joins the family). Adaptive reuse can be achieved by:

- Chunking designs, code, or data to extract multiple functions or views of the data
- Combining designs, code, or data into higher-level, reusable functions or databases
- Generalizing an existing part or component into a reusable design, module, or database
- Customizing designs, code, or data to prepare them for a specific application or environment

Chunking helps identify the different functions or data woven together in a module or database. These can then be separated and reused. Data normalization, for example, progressively chunks data down into its component groupings.

Combining these elemental units into higher-level organs or organisms enables us to reuse the power and elegance of the smaller parts to create even more powerful reusable components.

Generalizing lets us look at two or more similar yet different functions or data structures and observe their similarities. Once we know how they are alike we can create higher-level abstractions that allow us to reuse the basic principles. In object-oriented programming, for example, we can define a class of objects called *door* which has hinges, latches, and states of being open or closed. We can then reuse these abilities to describe car doors or house doors or even hoods and trunks.

Customizing, however, invites us to look at how the function or data is different and unique. Continuing the door example, we could define classes of doors for hoods, trunks, and car doors that specify their unique function or application.

Regardless of how we identify and create a reusable component— design, code, data, or test case—we will need some way to store and retrieve it on demand.

REUSE REPOSITORIES

Component repositories are a form of long-term ''memory'' that facilitate reuse. They encounter initial success and enthusiasm as people begin to add parts to the repository. Difficulties occur when these same people are called on to reuse the components in the library. Initial components may lack the robust functionality required to ensure reuse. As a result, there will be some technical difficulties in applying reuse to achieve customer needs. This is okay because there is no failure, only feedback. These early components can be evolved into important members of the reuse repository. To encourage reuse, programmers and analysts should be challenged to argue their use or avoidance of reusable components during an inspection or walkthrough.

Reusable designs increase the possibility of code reuse and make the resulting programs more maintainable. Strict focus on reusing designs, however, can cause designers to overlook better alternatives. Use your common sense; reuse what is reusable.

Program generators capture similarities among applications and apply knowledge at higher conceptual levels. Fourth generation languages do the same thing. They are a powerful tool in the hands of a prototyper who has access to a reusable repository of data, information, and knowledge about the business.

Reuse opportunities vary with the class of system and its environment. Ground-breaking new systems will initially have fewer reuse opportunities than existing, known application domains. Japanese software houses, for example, reuse up to 80 percent of existing application software when creating a custom configuration for a customer. Creating space station software, however, is a less understood application domain; reuse may be more difficult. You can measure the value of reuse by counting every incident of reuse. It costs more to set up a reuse program initially, and then it begins to repay itself over time. The Japanese SIGMA project has allied over a hundred different companies to produce reusable components for the Unix environment. Toshiba's Heavy Apparatus Engineering Lab uses real-time Fortran for 60 percent of its reusable code and is moving toward the C language for the remainder. GTE Data Services uses COBOL and assembly because of the transaction processing nature of their business (Gruman 1988).

Reuse can occur anywhere in the software process—from project plans to design documents, from code to data, from test cases to user training. Figure 6.2 shows the reuse pyramid. The foundation of most effective busi-

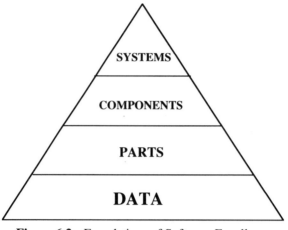

Figure 6.2   Foundations of Software Excellence

ness oriented reuse strategies is data. By creating pools of shared data, prototypers can begin to leverage their work with each successive application created. These pools (Figure 6.3) also provide a strategic resource for users to evaluate their customer base, identify new markets, be more responsive to changes in market conditions, and counter competitive threats. One of the reasons that the ''information center'' concept never caught on was that the data for one of these was often spread across dozens if not

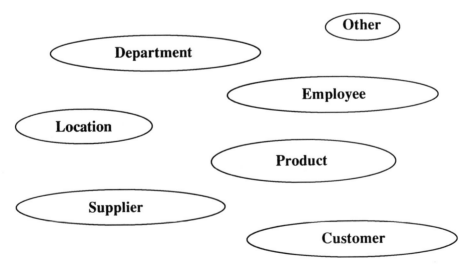

Figure 6.3   Data Reservoirs

hundreds of applications. This is another reason that executive support or decision support systems, which are vital to the strategic health of the organization, have had a hard time getting started and delivering return on investment.

[Data] is an open system . . . that learns from its experiences. It has adaptive mechanisms. . . . It is, in a sense, organic.
— *Dan Appleton (1983)*

This philosophy of shared data pools often seems strange to those of us brought up with structured programming and data flows. To be successful at rapid evolutionary development, most of your data can't flow; it must remain in one place where people can use and reuse it. It can be managed and duplicated where required. It can be syphoned off, transformed, and streamed into other pools. In event-driven, real-time systems, this obviously isn't so, but in application creation it is.

Another advantage of data pools (i.e., tables or databases) lies in the ability to create and maintain and share documentation and training in their use. Then, with this foundation to stand on, prototypers can create reusable parts to access and process the raw data into forms more suitable for human consumption. Data pools simplify the development of the processing required to meet a customer's needs—another advantage of creating the data first.

The data pools in Figure 6.3 form a more object oriented (Figure 6.4) or information engineering (Figure 6.5) strategy for software creation. Customers, for example, would know their own names, addresses, phone numbers, and so on. They might also know what kind of products or services they buy on a regular or irregular basis, and how much money they have to spend. This object orientation can benefit rapid evolutionary developers because it focuses on organisms and organizations and elements of the total system and can be implemented in any language, not just object oriented ones.

Object oriented designs and language use much of evolutionary theory—similarities are passed on through inheritance from a common ancestor or "super class" to a subclass and finally to a single "instantiation" of an individual. Object oriented systems also use:

- Data abstraction (rather than functional decomposition) to design systems
- Information hiding to distance the system from its environment
- Dynamic binding to allow for maximum flexibility at run time

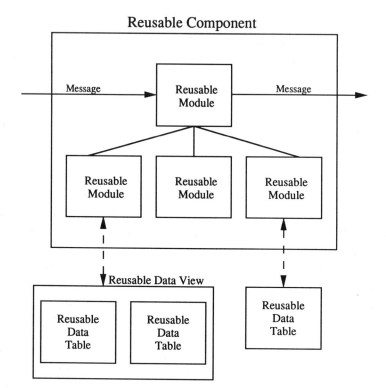

Reusable Component

Message

Reusable Module

Message

Reusable Module

Reusable Module

Reusable Module

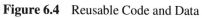

Reusable Data View

Reusable Data Table

Reusable Data Table

Reusable Data Table

Figure 6.4 Reusable Code and Data

	Data	Process
Conceptual	Business Modeling Strategic Systems Planning	
Logical	Logical Data Modeling	Systems Planning Systems Architecture
Physical	Physical Data base Design Populated Data Structures	Module Design Executable Code

Figure 6.5 Information Engineering Approach

Data abstraction is a way of looking at data in terms of its purpose and abilities. Customer data, for example, serves the purpose of representing each customer and their actions. Information hiding obscures each module's internal processing and data from the outside world. Just as you cannot know *how* I'm thinking as I write this, you can read *what* I've written. Dynamic binding allows each module or object to remain free until it is called during the system's processing. Dynamic binding uses message passing to allow flexibility in how objects interact. A customer *object*, for example, could tell a company *object* to connect a service. The company, in turn, could tell the service *object* what was needed and inform the accounting and billing *objects*. Dynamic binding and messaging encourage flexibility.

Once the data is created in an object oriented way, prototypers can then begin creating parts (or methods as they are called in object oriented design) to add, change, delete, or access the data in useful ways. These programs or modules are often simple and widely reusable by any application that needs them. From these one-celled, one-function parts, prototypers can compose higher-level components or organs that perform more complex analysis and transformation of the data into information.

And, at the highest level, whole applications can be reused. Most application developers, for example, take the operating system, network, and database system software for granted, but they are an example of high-level reuse.

Regardless of which reuse level interests people the most, the most important key to rapid evolutionary development is data.

REUSING DATA

Throughout time, evolution seems to take forever. Insects, however, evolve quickly to deal with pesticides through their rapid generational turnover, which provides massive and frequent opportunities for genetic recoding. The rapid rate of human evolution, however, depends on our ability to change and adjust our conceptual, logical, and physical worlds to our needs. Rather than change the human organism, we change the programs we put into the biocomputer we call a brain (training) and we extend the reach of our physiology through the use of machines—cars, planes, boats, rockets, or computers. Satellites in space vastly extend our ability to see changes on the planet. Our personal evolution grows each time we expand our understanding of the world. In this way, we change without having to resort to genetic mutation and natural selection. Data evolves in much the same way as human knowledge, by learning as it grows. As we add data to a database, the information or knowledge contained in that database increases like the mind of any child.

Data-driven prototyping develops and maintains open, shared databases that can constantly be extended to accommodate new information requirements. Reusable data will need to be normalized. Over the years, several genetically advanced forms of data have appeared—normal forms. First normal form simply deals with establishing a consistent number of fields per record, all of the same size. Second and third normal forms introduce *key* fields and their relationships to other nonkey fields. Second normal form ensures that all nonkey fields relate to the entire key. Third normal form ensures that no nonkey field relates to another nonkey field. Fourth normal form ensures that a record contains no more than one independent, multivalued field. Fifth normal form simplifies things even more by creating smaller groups of data from which larger, more complex groups of information can be derived.

Using this model as the basis of creating and growing evolutionary software systems, we can begin to see that we must have ways of storing our models of the world in such a way that it can be changed easily. You can change your mind, but can you change your software? Typically not very easily, because the knowledge is hard coded into the program or inflexible data structures. Through proper use of data, evolution becomes a process of changing the data stored in databases, not genetically re-engineering the software system. The database, like the human mind, can code, store, and retrieve data, generate decisions, and much more. Successful data design is the foundation of evolution and reusability.

There are three levels for data architecture: a conceptual or enterprise level, a logical or functional level, and a physical level.

Just having the right data and information can have a strategic impact because it will enable customers to identify new markets, evaluate trends, and increase sales through the application of ''end-user'' tools for database analysis.

The technical, physical, and political barriers to data can be a major roadblock in the rapid evolutionary development of any project. For prototyping to succeed, the prototyper must have access to any and all data, regardless of how far back in the woods it may be.

For data to be as reusable as possible, IS prototypers must use the same name for data elements with as few synonyms as possible. Unfortunately, during English classes in school, some teacher instilled in students that repeating the same word over and over again would be boring for the reader. Bore me! Especially in computer programs. Bore me! Make it easy for me. Simple subject, simple verb, and simple object: MOVE COLORADO TO STATE, and then simply refuse to give COLORADO and STATE more exotic names. Bore me!

REUSING PROCESSING

There are many levels at which reuse can be achieved. Fred Brooks suggests three levels (Gruman 1988): algorithm, code component, and design reuse. Algorithms validate fields such as employee and customer names and numbers and crunch arithmetic calculations. Code components can update databases, communicate with users and other systems, and process specific types of application problems. For example, the Common Ada Missile parts, a generalized cruise-missile guidance system that uses Ada packages, has been widely reused (Gruman 1988). At Toshiba's Heavy Apparatus Engineering Lab, the reuse rate is 55 percent of delivered code. The challenge for reusable components is to create ones that can do a lot of work, but also be flexible enough for broad application and reuse to defray the cost of creating them. Design reuse takes software up a level of abstraction such that a design can be tailored and delivered in any software or hardware domain. Compared to code or algorithm reuse, design reuse offers the flexibility to choose hardware and software platforms. Design reuse begins at the system's conception. Prototypers must constantly be on the alert for an opportunity to create or reuse portions as they chunk the system into subsystems and components. Early identification of reusable design pieces also tends to result in the creation of reusable code components.

At the lowest level, module designs and code can be *adapted* to work with new data. This implies genetic re-engineering of the element or cell to allow for evolutionary growth and development. In evolutionary terms, this is known as adaptive radiation—the rapid divergence of many new forms of life from some common ancestor. Although a valuable way to reuse software, it creates problems because:

1. It can propagate defects to a wide range of components
2. It creates new parts that have to be maintained

At the next level, data tables, databases, software modules, and documentation are used *as is*. This *cellular* approach maximizes the benefit of any given part. Nothing need be changed. The only drawbacks to this approach are:

1. Changes to the part can impact many applications and requires extensive testing
2. The part can try to be all things to all users and eventually fail to be of value to any
3. It may be difficult for prototypers to evaluate which parts offer the right features for their application

At the next higher level, a more object oriented level, data and processing combine into reusable components that perform higher-level functions. At this level, the component acts like an organ in the body, processing specific inputs and developing specific outputs. As a prototyper moves toward higher-level reusable components, the value of each instance of reuse increases and the number of times a component can be reused decreases because it becomes more specific. The more stable the data pool, the more likely it becomes that major reusable components can be created.

At the highest level, whole applications can be reused. This is similar to cloning whole organisms. In Japan, software houses provide custom systems from reusable applications. Banking applications, for example, are created for one customer and then customized for each additional customer. Because the core of the processing is reusable, the custom features can be added at a low cost, maximizing customer satisfaction and profit per system. Comparing this to our biological example, there are similarities among different races of humans and useful specializations as well.

At this high level of reuse, reusable documents and training can assist in delivering the maximum productivity and quality with minimal cost. This is how software houses make a profit, through development and continuous reuse of existing components and applications. This is why so many companies are writing software for desktop computers; the opportunities from reuse on a grand scale reduce the cost per copy to a level that almost anyone can afford.

Fred Brooks (Gruman 1988) said that "in Unix, the power of the whole pipes-and-filters and unified files structures . . . lets people lash together pieces they have lying around. These kinds of reusability are immediate." Having used Unix extensively in the 1970s and 1980s, I can agree.

Programming in the Unix Shell can teach you a lot about reusability. I liked it so much that I wrote a book about it (Arthur 1990).

Types of Reusable Processing Modules

There are six (7 − 1) key kinds of business processing modules:

1. Data gathering: getting input for the process
2. Data storage: updating data in memory or magnetic media
3. Data processing: converting the raw data into information or knowledge
4. Data retrieval: selecting stored data and information
5. Data presentation on various media
6. Communication

Data gathering modules include user and system interfaces. Data storage modules take the gathered data and store it in appropriate databases. Processing modules transform the raw data into information and knowledge. Data retrieval modules include queries and extracts for reports. Data presentation modules include reports and screens. Communication modules connect the system with its external and internal components.

At minimum, these reusable software modules should have the qualities of being general, flexible, reliable, modular, simple, and self-documenting. Generality implies that the module is usable in many circumstances. Flexible modules evolve easily. Reliable modules rarely fail. Modular components have a single entry and exit point, and perform a single function. This singularity brings about simplicity (7±2 decisions). These modules also document their abilities through clear use of the programming language, data names, and comments.

Unfortunately, most of today's programmers tend to subtly encode specific information about the operating environment—operating system, database, hardware, and interfaces—into modules. To enhance their reliability, modules should be as independent of the data as possible. Using "information hiding," the structure and origin of the data can be hidden from the module's processing. Reusable modules may also practice "mutual suspicion"; this paranoid practice ensures that the data passed from some other module is valid before using it. Other fault-tolerant practices can be employed to trap errors when they occur and exit gracefully.

Language Choice

As you think about developing reusable software, delay the choice of a language as long as possible. Then implement the reusable components in the most flexible language for the task.

Fourth generation languages (4GLs) rely on predefined procedures that may or may not be appropriate for the application. 4GLs may also break down under high volume processing. They are interpretive, not compiled; they simply may not be able to carry the load. 4GLs are, however, an excellent choice if the language matches the customer's problem.

It may be necessary to abandon a 4GL when the customer's requests exceed the predefined limits of the language; you can then move into a third generation language (3GL). 4GLs take time to learn because there are no real standards for how they work. Each is different and some are complex. SQL (structured query language), for example, has a complex syntax that rivals IBM JCL (Job Control Language). The costs of learning the language may eat the savings in development time. For example, I used ORACLE to create a reuse catalog and found it easy to create the basic data and screens, but then as I began to iterate to customize the system, I ran into difficulty with all of the rules for triggering processes. Programmers may also attempt to use the 4GL in a 3GL way and run into problems. 4GLs require a different development mind set.

When it comes to productivity, if we measure it in terms of executable lines of code per staff month, 4GLs may appear to be more productive. One study (Misra 1988) found that 4GL implementations required one-third less statements than a comparable 3GL. Most of this reduction was in the data declarations required.

Any language can be used to prototype almost any kind of application. 3GLs offer the broadest trained programming work force. It may take a little longer to accomplish a prototype in a 3GL, but it will be more efficient and potentially more effective because it can be customized to the user's ultimate specifications. And then again, it may not take as long to do a prototype in a well known and understood 3GL because the prototyping team has more experience and training in its use, and there are more productivity tools to support it. Thirty years of evolution has improved languages such as COBOL, C, Pascal, Fortran, and PL/I to the point where a programmer can readily identify the data structures and the common structured programming constructs—if, case, while, until, and sequential—making each new language easier to learn.

Object oriented languages offer tremendous capabilities for implementing user interfaces. Object oriented windowing packages such as X Windows, Motif, NextStep, OpenWindows, Windows, DecWindows, Mac-Multifinder, and Presentation Manager can be accessed from 3GLs to allow flexible use of both object oriented languages and 3GLs to meet the technical needs of the prototype and the business needs of the customer. Also, object oriented designs can be implemented in 3GLs to maximize application flexibility.

Application generators offer some of the best and worst of both worlds. Application generators turn designs into 3GL that can be compiled for efficiency of operation. Generators typically deliver not only code but documentation as well. Some even create test cases for the generated code. Generators deliver fast, effective systems quickly, but the generated code can be painfully difficult to change or customize unless the prototyper works at the design level. This is good because we want prototypers to work at the highest conceptual level possible and bad because we may want to customize the system, ultimately, to the user's full requirements.

REUSABLE DOCUMENTATION

Looking at the coding process as the only place to reuse things is often shortsighted. If, as Capers Jones (1987) suggests, paperwork is 25 percent of the total effort in a software project, then documentation is another great place to generate a return on investment by creating everything from boilerplate to complete documents that can be reused to provide:

1. Requirements for similar applications or portions (e.g., security, reporting, error handling)
2. Designs: system and detailed designs
3. Plans: project management, test plans, quality assurance plans
4. Methods and procedures: design and testing methods and procedures
5. User guides

REUSABILITY TOOLS

The most innovative and successful software creation in the 1990s will be done by organizations that have specialized tools like the reuse catalog and reusable, evolutionary components and computing abilities that match their business. The Japanese Sigma project has three major design principles for reusability tools (Akima 1989):

1. Let users create an optimal integrated environment for their needs
2. Promote technology transfer through use
3. Encourage development of future third-party tools that can be integrated or used to replace or mask existing reusability tools

Some of Sigma's existing tools include documentation, networking, and project management tools. Project management tools include the PDCA cycle for continuous quality improvement. There are over 40 Sigma tools consisting of 2 million lines of C code. Other tools include integrated screen, form, file, and database design tools.

The Sigma design environment consists of 32-bit workstations with powerful networking functions, resource sharing functions, advanced user interface, and the minimum resources needed to run the Unix-like OS and Sigma tools.

Central Software Repository and Catalog

Reuse can begin immediately. Many small, one-celled modules and databases can be created as projects develop. These can be added to the ever growing wealth of software in the repository. As projects grow and mature, other larger components differentiate and grow from the smaller pieces. Readymade tissues and organs—menuing, graphics, application libraries—can spawn from the creation process. These various components can be created to be portable across computing systems to facilitate rapid and inexpensive transition to new or additional platforms.

As the population of reusable components expands, we must be able to catalog and reuse information, ideas, and knowledge, as well as various software parts and components. An effective and efficient cataloging system is essential to successful software reuse. The reusable software repository or catalog should match the sophistication of the public libraries. Storing components is one thing, retrieving them is another. People think in ideas, concepts, and facts. The catalog should think in the same way. Most catalogs, unfortunately, are rigid; human minds are not. Prototypers should be able to tag and link components on the fly as they discover relationships. Prototypers may also want to add notes in the margin or bookmarks into the repository so that they can return to a reference after they have finished looking around. The catalog can also enable a user to navigate through the webs of reusable components demonstrating connections and interactions.

Prototypers need a rapid method for identifying available candidates for reuse (Figure 6.6). If it takes too long, they will turn to creating the parts all

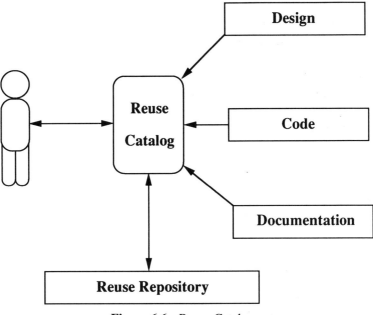

Figure 6.6   Reuse Catalog

over again. The model suggested by Prieto-Diaz and Freeman (1987) looks first at how one component is like another and then how they are different:

```
begin
   search library
   if identical match then select and terminate        (direct reuse)
   else
      collect similar components
      for each component
         compute degree of match
      end
      rank and select the best
      modify component to fit                           (adaptive reuse)
   endif
end
```

For information, knowledge, designs, code, and data to be accepted into the repository, it will need to pass the following tests:

```
if an object is
   hardware independent and
   software independent and
   general and
   modular and
   self-documenting
then
   it is reusable
endif

If the object
   fits the business model and
   fits the architecture and
   is reusable
then
   it can go in the repository
endif
```

PROBLEMS

There are several reusability issues. How much will it cost to save money with reuse? How much will it improve productivity? How do I estimate return on investment? What are the employee incentives and barriers to reuse?

Roadblocks to reuse include the not-invented-here (NIH) syndrome, whisky (WISCY—Why isn't Sammy coding yet?), and the investment in learning and understanding reuse. Training designers and programmers to use the reuse repository costs time and money. Tracking usage of components makes configuration management costs higher. Elevating the creativity level to the design or requirements stage, and rewarding early product delivery will often knock down these roadblocks.

Reusable components cost more to build, test, and document, but you can use them repeatedly in endless variations. Reuse dramatically reduces the time required to create and deliver a system. Reuse increases confidence in estimates and allows for ongoing evolution of requirements.

The technical problems of creating, cataloging, and recovering components are complex. Noboru Akima, planning director of the Japanese Sigma (reuse) project (Gruman 1988), said that "these problems are exactly the ones that prevent the idea from realization. . . . It [is] difficult to define the component size, interface, and functionality."

Programmer productivity, if measured in terms of just lines of code produced, tends to punish groups that reuse code extensively. Prototypers will generate less code and reuse more. One way to overcome this is to measure total functionality delivered in *function points* or to include all instances of reuse in the productivity calculation.

Some languages, COBOL specifically, do not encourage modularity, but rather encourage large, ever expanding programs consisting of dozens to hundreds of paragraphs that, because of their custom nature, are difficult if not impossible to reuse.

Reuse is most effective at solving routine common problems. Within the confines of known application domains, reuse offers great potential. New application domains, however, require innovative solutions. Innovative designs, by their very nature, will require innovative approaches which may or may not be able to leverage the existing base of software components. At best, innovative solutions will be able to use the most basic elements of software, but possibly not the larger components.

Reuse is still struggling to establish itself in environments where the underlying technology is changing rapidly. COBOL or Fortran, for example, are stable and relatively unchanging. In parallel processing environments, however, reuse may be difficult initially. Rapid technological changes require more innovation and risk.

Rewarding Reuse

To succeed at reuse, you will need to reward its application. Employee incentives for reuse are somewhat intangible unless you make it tangible by rewarding both reuse and the creation of reusable components. Some companies have instituted a royalty program for reused components and parts.

GTE Data Services prints a quarterly newsletter describing benefits and success stories, offers $50 rewards for programmers whose components get reused each year, and makes successful reuse part of a project manager's job evaluation (Gruman 1988).

SUMMARY

The prototyper's job becomes easier as we learn to take advantage of reusable data, processing, and documentation. Reusable components may take a little longer to create, but they will serve the corporation for many years, perhaps even decades as they grow and evolve. Vast improvements in productivity are possible when we adopt a mind set that we will reuse what is reusable and create new reusable components where none were previously available.

To maximize the benefits from rapid evolutionary development, reusability has to be one of the arrows in your quiver.

CHAPTER 7

User Interfaces

A recent survey indicated that one-third to one-half of the people surveyed in countries like the United States, Canada, several European countries, Australia, and the United Kingdom have ''trouble'' operating a computer (INC. 1991). User interfaces are a major cause of this difficulty. The real user interface includes everything the user works with—manuals, training, as well as the screens and reports. This chapter will not and cannot hope to teach you everything you need to know to develop wonderful user interfaces. It can help you understand the benefits of user interfaces and the pivotal role they play in rapid evolutionary development.

Eighty percent of customer satisfaction comes from the user interface. Usable systems let users do their jobs quickly, accurately, and enjoyably. One of the major problems with most systems is that the user interface is clumsy, painful, and frustrating. We need user-seductive interfaces that draw people into using the system regardless of how much they are attached to the old system or method. In 1975, when they first installed video terminals and IBM's window to MVS—TSO, programmers came in at all hours of the day, night, and weekend to use the biggest revolution since the punch card. The same thing happened when Apple introduced the Lisa, which later became the Macintosh. The windows, icons, mouse, and pointer were irresistible. User interfaces can enhance or kill a system.

There are no design strategies that guarantee the resulting interface will be easy to learn or use. The only way to create these interfaces is by creating and testing them rapidly, and then modifying the design based on user feedback. Because interface development is based on insufficient knowledge, rapid prototyping is the key to almost every phase of interface development. Prototyping allows you to make the interface available for early user testing and evolutionary refinement. Modular implementation of user interfaces benefits the prototyping staff, the evolution and maintenance staff, and the customer. This separation of application and interface allows the project to empower a user-interface specialist to work directly on customer requirements. This interface specialist can begin working immediately on designing the interfaces without having to wait on a precise functional specification. Design the human factors of the interface first, then add in the functionality as it becomes more clearly defined. Design and prototyping of the user interface begins the process of gathering customer requirements and sheds light on the functionality that will need to be behind the interface to make the system valuable in the customer's eyes. The benefits of modular user interfaces (Figure 7.1) include:

- Reduced prototype development time
- Higher productivity
- Higher quality
- Improved ability to develop complex functionality
- More consistent user interfaces
- Applications that are easier to learn and use

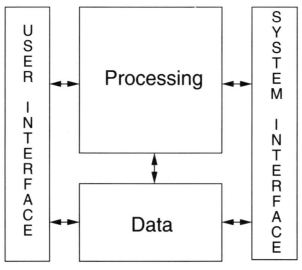

Figure 7.1   Modular User Interface

Iterative design and prototyping of the user interface (Figure 7.2) allows for flexibility in all stages of development, which in turn causes fast turn-around, customer enthusiasm, and the creation of a superior system. To succeed at user interface development, we must implement a *deliverable* user interface prototype. Using information hiding to separate the interface from the processing will simplify maintenance and evolution.

Writing and debugging user interfaces become simpler by the application of object oriented techniques. In many cases, windowing software already exists (e.g., the Macintosh Developers' Toolkit and X-Windows in Unix). Prototypers can reuse facilities like menu bars, icons, and points to maximize productivity and quality while ensuring consistency in the user interface. Even when developing an interface from scratch, separation of the interface from the application encourages consistency and reusability of the modules and data required, while allowing for ease of testing and verification.

If you standardize the way user interfaces work across all applications, you will simplify the creation of reusable components to accomplish these missions. Users benefit from not having to learn one way on this system and one way on another. After years of using IBM personal computers, for example, I was delighted to discover that the command to quit an application on the Macintosh was *always* in the File menu bar and always available from the keyboard by the key combination, *Command-Q.* Consistent, common interface facilities and commands will allow customers to become much more productive over time.

For maintainers another advantage of standard user interfaces comes when it's time to give existing applications a face lift or when one interface is needed to multiple systems (Figures 7.3 and 7.4). In many instances, customers don't want a whole new system. Instead, they really want a better interface to their existing systems. In other cases, they have two

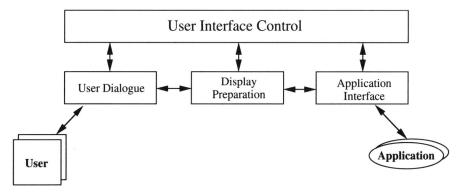

Figure 7.2 User Interface Design

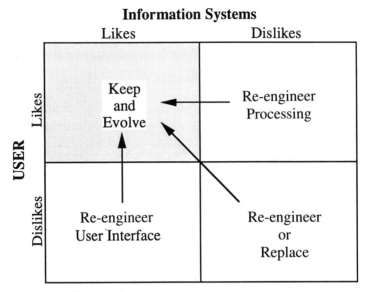

Figure 7.3 Re-engineering User Interfaces

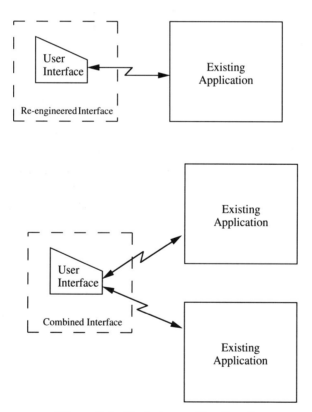

Figure 7.4 Evolutionary User Interfaces

systems that were built independently without regard to their relationship. A simple way to observe this is to wander around the customer's site and notice how many different terminals there are on a user's desk or in a given area. If there is more than one and each is running a different application, odds are good that they could benefit from combining access to these systems into one interface application.

Separation of the interface from the application allows evolutionists to improve the interface independent of the application and conversely to improve the application independent of the interface. Making enhancements and repairs becomes less risky because the change will be isolated to either the interface or the application, reducing the chance of contaminating one or the other with an incorrect change.

Users benefit from rapid evolution of their initial uncertainties into demonstrable user interface prototypes and from the ease of learning in well-designed interfaces. Separation of interfaces from the application can also allow the creation of multiple interfaces to the same system to support different customers or clients. For example, the interface required for large customers may be more complex than for smaller customers served by different marketeers. This flexibility flows over into customization of user interfaces to meet specific needs; the same system with a custom interface may be able to serve different customers. Japanese software houses use this approach to reuse the core of their applications like banking and then customize the interfaces to meet the needs of different customers. *Custom* is the key part of the word *customer*. Customer satisfaction will depend on the ability to customize the system to their needs rather than attempting to achieve the ''one size fits all'' model of the world. Even cars come in different models and with different options. Software must do the same.

Successful applications of the future will allow the user to customize as many features as possible. In most desktop computers, users can customize the colors and other features of the interface. Individuality is a prized possession and can be leveraged in user interfaces by giving up control and putting it in the hands of the customer.

COMMON FEATURES AND GOALS

No one designs a user interface from scratch anymore. Instead, you can reuse components of other successful interface designs—windows, icons, mice, and pull-down menus. Separate the user interface from the application. Either have the application call the user interface or the user interface pass data to the application, but don't intertwine the two. Chaos will result.

Having the user interface drive the interaction will simplify future changes because any redesign of the user interface will have little or no impact on the application.

A variety of capabilities will be useful in all user interfaces (Figure 7.5): validation, context-sensitive help, undo, tracking of operational sequences to gather user strategies, improve, and automate them, data collection of events and errors, and error messaging.

User interfaces share common goals. User interfaces need to be:

- Easy to use
- Easy to learn
- Easy to remember
- Easy to customize
- Easy to maintain
- Fast and fun

It seems that the easier an interface is to learn and use, the more difficult it is to create and maintain. There are a variety of common concepts included in powerful user interfaces:

- Direct manipulation (e.g., clicking and dragging windows and objects around) interfaces are a challenge to create because they use extensive graphics, provide many ways to accomplish the same command, and give immediate feedback
- Immediate visual feedback
- Undo: All actions are reversible

Mouse

On-line documentation

On-line help

Hierarchial menus

Style--windows, icons, menus, and commands

User customization

Error handling

Compatibility of systems

Figure 7.5   Interface Capabilities

- Varying levels for varying users (e.g., from a pull-down menu to a control key sequence) for the beginning to the advanced user; beginning users need more guidance, while advanced users require much less
- Consistency within and between applications of all key functions (e.g., open, close, save, etc.); consistency reduces learning and thinking time
- Explorable paths (e.g., pull-down menus with undo capabilities): Every action has a clear effect and can be easily reversed
- Minimal actions required to do almost anything (e.g., selecting data from a spreadsheet using a mouse and then using a pull-down menu to have the application graph the data)
- Guidance available at each step along the way to simplify learning
- Record and playback features to observe the user's actual behavior as they use the system and as a means to develop on-line tutorials by capturing the behavior of expert users

USER INTERFACE MANAGEMENT SYSTEMS

The continuing emphasis on creating user interfaces that exercise our senses using visual and auditory messages will stretch the abilities of existing user interfaces. User interface management systems (UIMS) have undergone significant evolution. First generation UIMS prototyping tools delivered only facade and simulations of display managers, which were primarily used by programmers (Hix 1990). Subsequent generations are shown in Table 7.1. Future generations will be functional, usable, accessible, and supplemented with expert systems to aid interface designers who will have little programming knowledge.

A UIMS delivers both higher productivity and better quality interfaces. Apple's MacApp, for example, can reduce interface development time by a factor of four (Shmucker 1986). The goals and advantages of a UIMS are to:

- Improve interface developer's productivity by removing programming role
- Improve resulting interfaces

A UIMS results in better interfaces because it can be created, tested, and evolved quickly. An interface prototyper can easily investigate various alternatives for the "look and feel" of the interface, iterating until a good solution emerges.

A UIMS offers better quality software at higher productivity. If we compare user interface development using standard programming tools with a UIMS environment, a UIMS will increase productivity. The code will be more flexible and maintainable because it is separate from the application code. It will also be more reusable because it uses the tools of the UIMS. The software will be more reliable because it was generated using the UIMS toolkit. If you want to learn how to reduce the cycle time for software development, take a look at your interface prototyping facilities.

Screen design facilities should include: interactive layout, dynamic field naming and editing, windows and scrolls, error handling, and documentation.

TABLE 7.1 User Interface Management System Evolution and Capabilities

Generation	Capabilities
First	**Mock-ups.** These early UIMSs consist of prototype builders and display managers that produce only mock-ups of the interface for subsequent development in the target language. The user interfaces are often sequentially oriented, consisting of menus and screens.
Second	**Runtime support.** These UIMSs offer runtime support with prototyping facilities, but are limited in scope. These UIMSs often rely on state-transition diagrams and are used primarily by skilled programmers.
Third	**Improved functionality and flexibility.** These UIMSs include more design capabilities for prototyping—object oriented programming, windowing systems (e.g., X Windows), and support libraries—while retaining the runtime support. These interfaces include direct manipulation of the interaction and more complex graphics. They are still the province of the programming staff.
Fourth	**Improved usability.** These UIMSs begin to use expert systems in support of the non-programmer. This emerging generation uses evaluation and iterative refinement to improve usability. These UIMSs will be an integrated part of the IPSE.
Fifth	**Expanded functionality and usability** for sound, graphics, and human factors interface design that requires no programmer involvement.

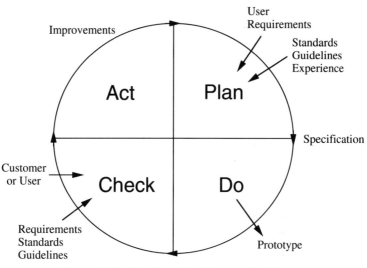

Figure 7.6   User Interface Prototyping Process

PROCESS

The process for creating a user interface follows another simple version of PDCA (see Figure 7.6):

- Select the type of dialogue to be carried out—command, menu, or graphics
- Determine the order of tasks to achieve a specific outcome
- Create a prototype or simulation
- Check the prototype of the user interface by having a user take it for a test drive
- Act to improve the interface based on feedback

Selecting the Dialogue

Current tools facilitate the communications of requirements, designs, and documentation through the use of text, tables, and graphics. This ignores some key human abilities, demonstrated by such simple systems as the Nintendo video games. User interfaces of the future will develop strength in the areas of:

1. Color
2. Tone (sound)

3. Motion
4. Three-dimensional representations
5. Vantage points (e.g., the "big picture")

Creating the Prototype

Creating a prototype will follow the process outlined in Chapter 5. Aside from this common process for prototyping, there are a number of techniques for designing and creating friendly user interfaces. More common techniques include:

1. Entering data only once
2. Displaying all necessary data required for user decision making
3. Providing a flexible method to control the sequence of screens
4. Using standard procedures wherever possible
5. Providing automatic security measures (e.g., prevent loss of work)

evaluating

Checking the Interface

If you don't enjoy criticism and feedback, user evaluation will kill you. If, however, you see it as an opportunity to improve, learn, and grow then you will create surprising customer loyalty. User evaluations of the prototype will reveal how your attempt to fulfill the user's desired map of the world was incorrect and must be improved. If the user is having trouble doing something, it is not because the user is stupid. There are no stupid users, only inflexible designers. To begin evaluating the user's needs:

1. Sketch out various scenarios on paper or using rough video
2. Write an initial user manual; have users play with it
3. Develop a mock-up or model; demonstrate it; put it where people can try it; and watch what works and what doesn't work
4. Hold contests to break the system or destroy it

My favorite technique for evaluating user interfaces mirrors the Wizard of Oz. This interface evaluation technique combines prototyping, simulation, and iterative testing. Like the Wizard of Oz, the system is configured so that inputs and outputs to the user can be monitored and manipulated by a prototyping wizard. By tracking the user's behavior and responding to it, prototypers discover how users interact with the system.

To evaluate how an interface and its supporting documentation can be improved, you can also:

- Measure the time required to perform an action or series of activities
- Count the number of errors made
- Count the number of requests for help
- Have users rate their satisfaction
- Have users describe their internal experience as they use the interface
- Videotape users' encounters with the system

SUMMARY

The creation of consistent user interfaces requires the attention of a user interface specialist. The human factors of interface design have evolved beyond the simple 25 by 80 line screens of the past to the graphical interfaces capable of color, sound, and motion. To maximize the productivity of the human element in any system, all of these facilities need to be brought into play.

CHAPTER 8

Software Evolution

In *The Mind and Nature*, Gregory Bateson's central theme states that evolution is a *mental* process. In essence, software is a reflection of the mental process of our customers and programmers. Software evolution involves both the physical and mental growth of the application system.

One-third to one-half the programming population is occupied maintaining and enhancing old code (DeMarco 1990). This explosion of evolutionists might be viewed as an overall success in achieving our initial mission: application creation. Successful automation is bound to increase the proportion of existing code to new.

Traditional manufacturing thought processes have produced 5–8 years as an expected average lifetime for software, but most large, established companies have millions of lines of code that are 15 years or older. From this we must infer that through growth and evolution, software systems secure their niche in the corporate environment. Once entrenched, replacing these systems becomes difficult and expensive, if not impossible.

Rather than cut the cost of software creation, we should increase the cost of software creation to reap significant decreases in evolution costs. Creating durable, reusable software is more expensive initially, but less costly over the long haul.

Once the initial version of the system has been created, there must be a way to evolve it toward the customer's ultimate goal. In this chapter, you'll discover the proven steps to software evolution that will allow you to take the system from infancy to adulthood. This process of continuous evolution is described in more detail in *Software Evolution—The Software Evolution Challenge* (Arthur 1988).

In many ways, software *evolution* fails to describe the daily activities of the hordes of programmers and analysts who work on existing software. They constantly change software to meet the evolving needs of the business, the application, and technology. In a typical environment, these people spend less than 10 percent of their time actually fixing defects. They spend the majority of their time on enhancements—software evolution. Maintenance means to preserve from failure or decline. Evolution means a continuous change from a lesser, simpler, or worse state, to a higher or better state. Given a choice, would you rather improve software or merely preserve it?

Because most organizations depend heavily on existing software systems, software evolution is a critical function. Supporting these systems is the mission of the software evolutionist.

To help you accomplish this mission, this chapter will:

- Explain the functions and flow of the software evolution process
- Define the three types of software evolution: corrective, adaptive, and preventive
- Identify the factors critical to successful, productive creation and evolution of software

FIRST STEPS

IS departments spend money on software creation and evolution in approximately the following amounts:

- 30 percent creation
- 70 percent evolution

Thus, if you want to reduce your costs, you must initially focus on the place with the most potential for gain—evolution. Some people mistakenly believe that once you replace a system you will eliminate the burden of keeping the system up-to-date with its environment. Ridiculous! You simply substitute a larger, more complex system with higher evolution costs for the old one. What you need is a strategy for improving, re-engineering, or replacing systems that optimizes the company's return on investment (see Figure 7.2).

Your goal should be to move all systems from a lesser, simpler, or worse state, to a higher or better state.

Evolution

Most IS organizations have no defined process for evolving their existing software. You need one. Now.

Furthermore, it is a widely accepted fact that 20 percent of the programs incur 80 percent of the costs. We must fix them. Successful software engineering organizations will implement a *re-engineering group* whose sole function is to restructure and re-engineer existing programs into easily maintainable units. You can do the same. Measured productivity and quality impact runs from 10–40 percent depending on the depth of re-engineering performed.

Creation

Most IS departments have bought and discarded several *creation* methodologies. What you need is an evolutionary methodology to start with and then a *process group* whose sole purpose in life is to continuously improve the creation and evolution methodologies.

You will also need an *estimation group* to estimate projects. Then you must listen to them; you can't squeeze 10 pounds of software into a 5 pound bag. Customers prefer to know how long it will really take instead of being blind sided by continuous schedule delays.

Every new project must generate and reuse at least 10 percent reusable software—designs, code, and data. We must shift from building everything from scratch to composing and growing systems from existing components. Reuse is like compound interest—each reusable data structure or software module or design document builds for our future. If we spend them instead of saving them, we mortgage our future. If we save them, they can build a nest egg for our competitive survival.

Change Management

Perhaps the key tool for both creation and evolution is a change management system. Think of it as the purchase order system that drives all work. The business is constantly changing. You must have a mechanism to support that evolution. Evolution projects most commonly need to manage their growth and evolution. Prototyping projects often experience continuous change in requirements and design that occur *after* the project has begun. Rapid evolutionary development helps manage this change and change management can assist the process.

Change management is also a strategic tool for client satisfaction. Open the system to clients so that they can directly request changes, check on the status of their requests, and contact application gurus directly via electronic mail. By linking customers directly to IS, as Peters (1987) suggests, you can win their confidence for years to come.

Change management also collects all of the information necessary to identify the 20 percent of the programs that generate 80 percent of the costs. It is key to a successful evolution strategy.

The major concern of software staffs today is how to maintain the existing portfolio of programs. Consider the following evolution problems:

1. Most computer programs are difficult and expensive to maintain.
   a. One Air Force project cost $75 per line of code to build and $4000 per line to maintain.
   b. Software evolution costs $300 billion per year worldwide and demand is rapidly increasing (Martin & McClure 1983).
   c. In the past 15 years the budget for evolution has increased from approximately 50 percent of the resources expended on application software to 70–75 percent.
   d. Each new creation project adds to the evolution burden; ''add little to little and you have a big pile!''
   e. End-user applications on micros, minis, and information centers will require evolution.
   f. Demand for evolution already exceeds the capabilities of most evolution organizations. In business, the user department is programming many of their new applications. If evolution is not managed and improved, demand will easily exceed available programming resources, both data processing professionals and end-users.
2. Software changes are poorly designed and implemented.
   a. Design documents are rarely examined and updated to reflect changes to the system.
   b. A carelessly planned system takes three times as long as estimated to complete; a carefully planned system takes only twice as long.
   c. Difficult-to-maintain systems are ultimately rewritten at great expense.

    d. The two years following the release of a new product are spent implementing enhancements to bring the system up to the user's *expectations*.

    e. Most major enhancements are so poorly understood and implemented that several additional releases are necessary to clean up the enhancement.

  3. The repair and enhancement of software often injects new bugs that must later be repaired.

To resolve these problems and manage the growing software inventory, improvements are needed in the skills and productivity of maintainers, and in the quality and effectiveness of their work. This text focuses on helping you accomplish these goals.

To begin with, maintainers and managers should recognize that:

- Not all system maintainers are created equal, but that they can be educated to equivalent skill levels.
- The difference between the best and worst performers is at least an order of magnitude.
- The reason for this disparity is a difference in the level of knowledge and skill, often referred to as *breakthrough* knowledge.
- The best performers can execute the key software evolution activities more effectively than their counterparts.
- No single activity, or area of expertise accounts for the differences.
- The key to evolution productivity is to do most things a little better or faster (Peters 1987).
- A little more knowledge and skill multiplied over many activities produces striking differences in performance.

Providing maintainers with the latest knowledge, skills, and techniques to achieve their mission by performing the key software evolution activities a little better will reap significant productivity and quality improvements.

This text describes techniques for resolving many of the problems previously discussed. It describes the methods, tools, and techniques to improve your productivity and the quality of the software being maintained.

Software evolution consists of the activities required to keep a software system operational and responsive after it is accepted and placed into production. These activities include:

- Correcting defects (maintenance)
- Enhancing software functionality (evolution)
- Improving the quality of existing software (evolution)

In general, these activities keep the system in sync with an evolving, expanding user and operational environment. Functionally, software evolution can be divided into these three categories: corrective, adaptive, and preventive. All of these activities occur during the software evolution life cycle.

SOFTWARE LIFE CYCLE

The software life cycle covers the period from conception to retirement of a given software product. There are many definitions of the software life cycle. They differ primarily in the classifications of phases and activities. One traditional model is shown in Figure 8.1.

As this figure shows, for many large software systems, only one-fourth to one-third of all life cycle costs are attributed to software creation. The lion's share of the effort and costs are spent in the operations and evolution. (Note that the percentages indicate relative costs.)

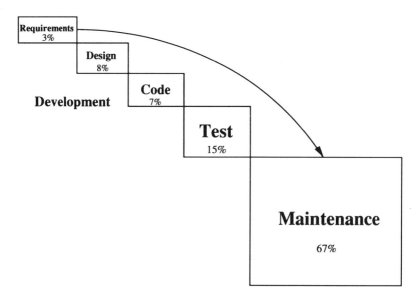

Figure 8.1 Waterfall Model

EVOLUTION AND DEVELOPMENT DIFFERENCES

While many activities related to creating and evolving software are similar, software evolution has unique characteristics of its own, including:

- *Constraints of an existing system.* Software evolution is performed on an existing production system. Any changes must conform or be compatible with existing architecture, design, and code constraints. Typically, the older the system, the more challenging and time consuming the evolution effort becomes. We need to understand how to prevent software extinction.
- *Shorter time frames.* Software creation may span one or more years, while evolution may span a few hours to cycles of 1–6 months.
- *Available test data.* Software creation creates all test data from scratch. Software evolution can use this existing test data and perform regression tests. Thus, the challenge is to create new data to adequately test the changes and their impact on the rest of the system.

Software evolution can and should be a structured process. It involves many different people and groups. Figure 8.2 illustrates the software evolution process. Figure 8.3 shows it in relation to the PDCA model.

EVOLUTION PROCESS

The evolution process begins when a request for change is initiated by a user. (Note that a user is defined as anyone who uses or interacts with the system, including systems engineers, information systems personnel, data processing, operations, or marketing personnel.) It ends when the system passes testing, is accepted by the user, and is released for operation. In between, a variety of activities involving maintainers, quality assurance, configuration management and test personnel must be planned for, coordinated, and implemented. These activities should be coordinated by use of change management.

Change Management

The basic objective of change management is to uniquely identify, describe, and track the status of each requested change. A change request provides the vehicle for recording information about a system defect, requested enhancement, or quality improvement.

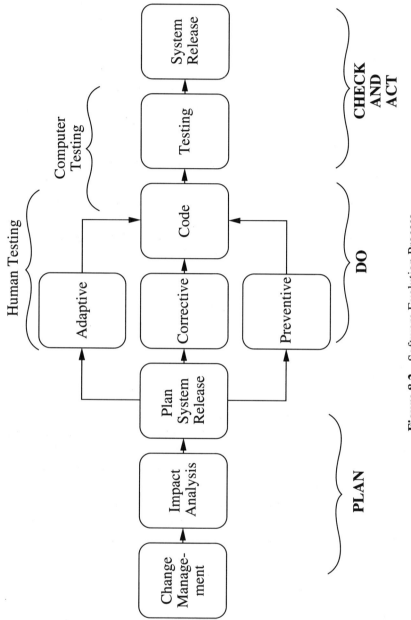

Figure 8.2 Software Evolution Process

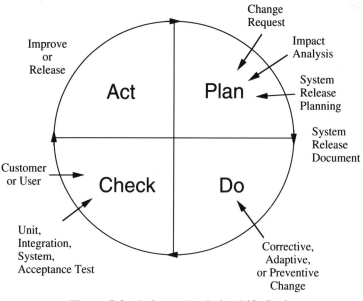

Figure 8.3 Software Evolution Life Cycle

The major change management activities are:

1. Entering change requests: Maintainers receive a request for some type of change (i.e., defect, enhancement, quality improvement), analyze the change, and generate a change request

   a. In this text, a system is defined as a group of programs (business environment) or configuration items (DOD environment)

   b. A program/configuration item is an executable piece of software made up of many modules or units

   c. A module is equivalent to a unit; it consists of object or source language code that, under the precepts of structured programming, implements a single function

2. Tracking change requests and providing regular and exception reports on the status of change requests

3. Providing an audit trail of changes

4. Providing input to project management and quality assurance systems

Impact Analysis

Once a change is initiated, an analyst has to evaluate its impact on the existing system and estimate the resources needed to complete the change. The overall objective of impact analysis is to determine the scope of the requested change as a basis for planning and implementing it.

The major impact analysis tasks are:

1. Evaluate change requests for potential impacts on existing systems, other systems, documentation, hardware, data structures, and humans (users, maintainers, and operators)
2. Develop a preliminary resource estimate
3. Document the scope of the requested change and update the change request

System Release Planning

Once these changes have been analyzed, they can be grouped together as a scheduled evolution release. This requires planning. The principal objective of system release planning is to determine the contents and timing of system releases.

The major system release planning tasks are:

1. Rank and select change requests for the next release
2. Batch the changes, by work product, and schedule the work
3. Prepare a system release planning document (Version Description Document for the Department of Defense) and place it under control of the configuration management system
4. Update approved change requests

When system release planning occurs varies depending on whether you work in a contractual or noncontractual environment. When evolution is done under contract, the contents and timing of a system release are negotiated and agreed to before any major work is begun, unless the contract is a "level of effort" contract.

Naturally, to agree on a contract, some level of analysis must be done to determine the scope of the changes and the resources required. When evolution is done without a contract (i.e., in-house), a release is planned after the change requests have been analyzed and the scope of work is clearly understood.

Once a release is planned, maintainers can design the change.

Making Changes

Corrective maintenance focuses on healing the system—fixing the defects. Using the construction or manufacturing paradigm, people who fix defects are *mechanics* or *maintainers*. This often demeaning title implies that programmers who maintain software like to ''get dirty.'' They tend to ''work with their hands'' and they are often undereducated.

If we use the evolutionary metaphor instead, we notice that the people who fix living systems are doctors. Doctors are typically highly trained, highly skilled men and women who work with their heads *and* hands. Doctors are usually well paid for helping their patients live a normal, productive life. Changing the metaphor of software will change how we view virtually every aspect of software creation and evolution.

Like living systems, software defects indicate that the system is not performing as originally intended, or as specified in the requirements. There are a variety of situations that can be described as corrective maintenance. Some of them include:

- Correcting a program that fails in the field or during testing (failures)
- Correcting a program that produces incorrect results (faults)

Corrective evolution is usually a *reactive* process. Defects generally need immediate attention. As most doctors will tell you, however, it is the excesses of our live-for-today life style that cause most problems. Like living systems, we have the option to help our software systems lead a more balanced life that will help the system live a long time.

Adaptive evolution includes all work related to changing how the software functions to meet the demands of its environment. Adaptive evolution includes system changes, additions, insertions, deletions, modifications, extensions, and enhancements. Adaptive evolution is generally performed as a result of new or changing requirements. Rapid evolutionary development can be used during the adaptive phase of software evolution to rapidly prototype major new enhancements to the system.

Some examples of adaptive changes include:

- Rearranging fields on an output report
- Changing a system to support new hardware configurations
- Adding a new function
- Deleting a function

• Converting a system from batch to on-line operation

Making a program more efficient does *not* affect its functionality. As a result, this type of change should be considered as part of preventive evolution.

Preventive evolution includes all efforts to improve the quality of the software. These activities can include restructuring code, creating and updating documentation, improving reliability or efficiency, or any other qualities. Some specific examples are:

• Improving efficiency, maintainability, or reliability *without* changing functionality
• Restructuring code to make it more maintainable
• Tuning a system to reduce response time

Although these three types of work are discussed separately, much of the work is performed concurrently. For example, enhancements and quality improvements are often worked and tested together. Design of one program's changes will overlap the coding of another's. All of these activities occur during the software evolution life cycle.

Coding

The objective of coding is to change the software to reflect the approved changes represented in the system (logical) program (physical) designs. The major coding activities are:

1. Implement and review all changes to code
2. Restore or place the source code under control of the configuration management system
3. Update the change request to reflect the modules or units changed

Testing

The next step in the evolution process puts the revised designs and code to test. The primary objective of testing is to ensure compliance with the original requirements and the approved changes. An incremental, evolutionary testing strategy will work the best. This kind of testing process weeds out bugs along the way, not when most of the work is done. The major testing activities are:

1. Human testing:
   a. *Walkthrough* or *inspection* requirements, designs, code, and data
2. Computer testing:
   a. *Unit test* all code changes by module or unit
   b. *Integration test* the interfaces between each module of the program and the program as a whole
   c. *System test* the interfaces between programs to ensure that the system meets all of the original requirements plus the added changes
   d. *Acceptance testing* where the user approves the revised system

System Release

Once a system has been thoroughly tested and accepted, it can be released for use. The objective of system release is to deliver the system and updated documentation to users for installation and operation.

The major activity associated with releasing a system is to package the release and send it to the user. System release packaging organizes all of the products of the evolution project—user manuals, software, data definitions, and job control language—for delivery to the client or user. System delivery methods vary from mail to floppy disks to telecommunications.

SOFTWARE EVOLUTION

Software evolution has been presented as a series of linear or sequential steps. There are, however, a number of activities that require overlaps and iterative loops. Some examples include recycling emergency repairs through the scheduled release process, returning change requests for clarification, additional analysis, and estimation after an impact analysis, and additional design and coding changes after testing discovers bugs. Usually, these processes occur synchronously throughout the evolution staff (e.g., systems analyst works on program design B while programmers revise the code in program A).

Although they may be handled loosely in some less crucial environments, the following factors are critical to effectively conducting software evolution:

- Develop and adhere to a well-defined and structured software evolution methodology; know when and how to tailor it to fit your environment

- Use structured design and coding techniques
- Control changes and software products with change and configuration management systems
- Conduct an impact analysis of all requested changes before agreeing to do them
- Establish scheduled releases and batch change requests to maximize productivity and quality
- Gather quality assurance data and use it to refine and improve software creation and evolution practices
- Use incremental testing to improve the quality of delivered software
- Introduce and use modern, automated tools to improve quality and productivity
- Obtain management's support for software evolution

SUMMARY

It is no secret that billions of lines of code execute every day in computers around the world. These systems are our cash cows, we've invested in their creation, we change them to meet the needs of the business, and they will be needed for years to come.

Existing systems have reached their position through evolution. Under the law of the jungle, existing systems have an advantage: all of the knowledge about the business is embedded in their logic. Replacement systems must rely on humans for this knowledge.

Where did these existing systems come from anyway? In business, they started as a seed to replace a manual procedure. Over the years, they grew, extending their roots into the heart of the business. Their shade and fruit nourished the business. Other systems sprang up to consume their data. Existing systems live in ecological balance with the decisions support systems they feed and their neighboring systems.

Replacement systems have no such support. Few software developers can build a replacement. Existing systems continue to grow and evolve while the replacement is being built. The replacement system does not have this advantage. Its requirements and designs are cast in stone. If the creation process takes longer than six months to a year, the replacement emerges from the swamp only to discover that it is already obsolete, and on the verge of extinction. Even if the replacement succeeds in suddenly replacing the existing system in a flash cut, it may harm or kill the rest of the environment. Successful replacement systems usually grow and evolve from a new seed. Replacement systems can also be purchased from vendors and transplanted into your environment.

Software re-engineering is an evolutionary process that educates software technicians, identifies candidates for re-engineering, genetically and structurally re-engineers them, and then sustains the improvements.

Software evolution consists of the activities required to keep a software system operational and responsive after it is accepted and placed into production. The key differences between evolution and creation are that:

- Rapid evolutionary development focuses on the fast creation and growth of an initial working system. Evolution continues the growth at a slower, more manageable rate.
- Creation happens in 7±2 months. Growth and evolution occur over the life of the system.
- Creation rapidly provides a working prototype or infant system. Software evolution ensures that it grows up in a rich environment safe from harm. Evolution consists of three key activities:
  - Corrective maintenance: fixing defects
  - Adaptive evolution: enhancing existing systems
  - Preventive evolution: improving software quality
- Creation freewheels through a fast, five-step PDCA process to create the system. The evolutionary process uses a longer, seven-step PDCA approach to changing software safely and ecologically. Those processes are:
  - Managing change
  - Analyzing impacts
  - Planning system releases
  - Making corrective, adaptive, or preventive changes
  - Coding changes
  - Testing changes
  - Releasing the system

Like having children, giving birth to a software system is only a small portion of the challenge. Keeping the system alive and growing to adulthood is a unique and interesting challenge that will consume most of the resources ever spent on the system. It pays to do it well.

CHAPTER 9

Metrics

The ability to measure has fueled virtually all of the past technological advances. Each new measurement has given us ways to extend our crude natural abilities to better measure height, width, depth, weight, texture, smell, temperature, and a myriad of other things in the realm of our senses. This is the major advantage of measurement—it enhances our ability to sense things not accessible to our native abilities and intelligence. Unaided, our brain takes in all of the data from the senses—sight, sound, smell, taste, and touch—transforming these crude impulses into measurements, which it then uses to estimate distances, dimensions, clarity, flavor, and so on.

Count what is countable, measure what is measurable, and what is not measurable, make measurable.

— Galileo Galilei

In physical science a first essential step in the direction of learning any subject is to find principles of numerical reckoning and methods for practicably measuring some quality connected with it.

— Lord Kelvin

The industrial revolution spawned the construction and manufacturing paradigms. Using these as models from which to base our search for software measurements, researchers have driven themselves (myself included) crazy. We've looked for ways to establish an estimating handbook like the ones builders have. We've focused measurement on ancient thoughts of production per worker hour. We've tried to find ways to make these other paradigms fit, but they just won't.

When we measure software using the construction paradigm, we end up focusing on due dates missed and little else. We punish programmers for doing the best they know how to do within the limits of the process they are using. When we measure software using the evolution paradigm, we end up with something else all together—an emphasis on quality and process improvement—because measurement is only a means to an end, not an end in itself.

So how do we measure software in such a way that it begins to help us rather than hinder us? Well when I was growing up, there was the door jamb of my room where I would stand and my mother would mark my height. Beside each mark, she would put the date, many of which were my birthday. Every year I could ''see'' how much I'd grown and the progress I was making toward adulthood. At the same time, my knowledge and skills were measured by progress through various grades of schooling.

I measured the growth and development of this book in the same way. Writing a book would be difficult if I had no measurement of progress toward completion. To keep myself sane, I measured its growth in words, pages, and chapters.

Measurement of growing things looks for increase in both size and ability. Measurement of growing things looks forward to birthdays, not to the day when the building can be torn down and replaced with a more gleaming, modern edifice, or an old car can be sold and another purchased to replace it. Measurement of software should celebrate the life and growth of the system, not a headlong rush toward obsolescence.

In its early years, we should expect rapid growth in size and ability in a given system. In the prototyping creation stage, similar to pregnancy, the software should grow rapidly from a concept into an initial working system. Then, once delivered, it can be nurtured and grown both mentally and physically. The human brain is full sized in early childhood. The brain is what allows the child to learn. In a software system, the databases and repositories of the system should be fully formed early in the system's life (3–5 years). Next, structural growth of most humans and systems will continue for several years and usually ceases in the late teens. From here on, systems may add more size and muscle, but the structure remains the same. Occasionally, systems will grow fat and require special assistance to regain their earlier trim. The true measure of human growth beyond the physical plane is the mental growth. Systems grow mentally through the evolution and addition of data. At some point, the physical development of a system will slow and the growth of its abilities will continue through the growth and evolution of its data, information, knowledge, and wisdom.

Measurement of growing systems also helps us detect and correct deficiencies *before* they become life threatening. There is an old story about a company that was having problems with the boilers in its plants. A special engineer was brought in to check the boilers. After listening to the groans and creaks for a little while, the engineer pulled out a ballpeen hammer and tapped a valve. Miraculously, the system began to hum again. The management was delighted and then they asked for the bill. The engineer asked for $300. "$300," they exclaimed, "but all you did was tap on a valve." The engineer nodded and told them that it was only a dollar for tapping on the valve, but $299 for knowing where to tap.

Metrics tell you where to tap. Measurement only serves to extend our abilities to understand the software process in ways invisible to the naked eye. Measurement is the *check* that precedes the identification and elimination of problems in the quality process. To reach the highest level in the SEI maturity framework—the highest step on the stairway to software excellence—you must be able to measure how your software grows and when it begins to diverge from the evolutionary tree.

Hitachi has been tracking productivity and defect rates for 25 years (Gross 1991). This massive database helps them determine how to improve their software process and how many people will be needed for a given project. Can you say the same?

ESTABLISHING MEASUREMENTS

As DeMarco (1982) has said, "What gets measured, gets done." Establishing measurements will take time and dedicated resources to design and develop the key metrics needed to track improvements in your process and results. As you might expect, there are four phases of establishing data collection and measurement: planning, doing, checking, and acting to improve.

Plan	1.	Setting the goals for measurement (Why are we collecting data?)
	2.	Modeling the process and data (What do we need to collect and when?)
	3.	Creating the measurement process, training, and tools
Do	4.	Implementing the entire measurement process

Check	5.	Evaluate the results of instigating measurements
Act	6.	Continuously improve the measurement process, tools, and training

Once you have a measurement process in place, you can begin to improve the software process. One recommended strategy for successful application of software measurement continues the use of PDCA:

1. Evolutionary Planning
   a. Collect data about the environment—resource usage, change and defect history, product dimensions, and other similar projects
   b. Define quality relative to the customer, project, and organization
2. Do
   a. Choose and tailor the software process, methods, and tools to satisfy the project goals
3. Check
   a. Analyze the data from other projects *before* starting the project
   b. Analyze data from the project as it proceeds
   c. Analyze the results after the project is finished
4. Act to improve
   a. Process
   b. Tools
   c. People

SETTING GOALS FOR MEASUREMENT

To establish goals for measurement, you will need to establish corporate goals first and then general IS objectives. Once these goals are chosen, you will need to set priorities for accomplishing each of these objectives. Once the goals, objectives, and priorities are known, it becomes much easier to select measurement methods and tools that will lead to the desired result.

1. Establish corporate goals. At Motorola, for example, the corporatewide direction is to achieve six-sigma level defects per unit (fewer than 3.4 in a million). This includes lines of code.
2. Develop general objectives. For each of the quality criteria such as

usability, maintainability, flexibility, and reliability, you will need specific, measurable objectives. For example, would your customer appreciate a fourfold increase in reliability? Probably. When it comes time to enhance the software, would you appreciate a tenfold increase in flexibility?

3. Set priorities. Which of the general objectives are the most important to long-term success and survival?
4. Match measurements to the prioritized objectives and select measurement methods and tools to carry them out with the minimal amount of effort.

MODELING THE PROCESS

Using the methodology of flow charting, identify the flow of the process. Then begin to identify how you intend to measure growth in size, complexity, and defects of the evolving system.

CREATING MEASUREMENTS

To actively manage productivity and quality, we need to know if they are improving or degrading. This implies the need for software metrics that track trends in software development.

Rules for successful measurement include:

- Make measurement beneficial for the person collecting the data
- Make measurement flexible to respond to custom requirements
- Define the process first, then the measurements
- Measure processes and verify them through feedback
- Define procedures for recognition, reward, and advice

The most common metrics of software *size* are function points and noncommentary lines of code. From these two metrics, it should come as no surprise that the two most common metrics for measuring productivity are function points per staff month and noncommentary lines of code per staff month. Function point measurement relies on the ''big picture'' of the system's behavior (Figure 9.1). Function point measurement has been largely a manual process, while lines of code can be easily automated. Productivity measurement of software evolution uses added, changed, and deleted functions or lines to indicate productivity.

Reuse of software data, documentation, and code dramatically affect

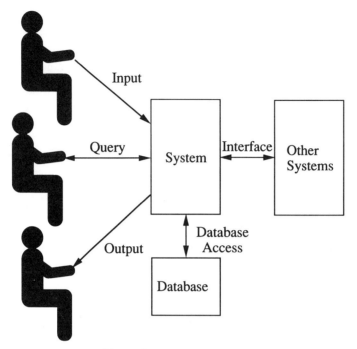

Figure 9.1 Program Types

productivity and quality. To factor reuse into your productivity equation, count:

1. How many times an object—data, design, documentation, code, or whatever—is reused
2. How many lines are in the module or data, and the number of times reused
3. How many function points are reused

Productivity metrics can help you understand whether the process changes are having the desired affect, but productivity metrics are also inherently dangerous *because* they will drive programmer behavior, even if it is counterproductive. You are much better off if you measure quality and let productivity take care of itself, because it will.

The most common metric of software quality is defects per thousand lines of code (KLOC). Current overall defect rates are 20–60 defects per 1,000 LOC. Delivered error rates are 1–10 errors per 1,000 LOC (Mills 1987). This is a good metric for determining the capability of your coding and testing processes, but it misses the requirements and design stages where 60 percent of all defects enter the process.

Defects per thousand lines of code is a useful internal measure, but less useful for measuring how customers feel about the system. You can have a very low defect rate and also have very unhappy customers. To better understand customer dissatisfaction, you can measure mean time between failures or response time or some other measure of the customer's direct experience of the system.

The next most common software metric is complexity, measured using McCabe's CC. It has been widely established as described in Chapter 2 that modules with a CC of 10 or less have no defects and that modules of complexity greater than 50 are unmaintainable. This implies an inescapable cost as the module's complexity rises above 10.

To maximize quality of each module, you should attempt to build modules with a CC of 7±2 (5–9). This "target value" will minimize the cost of software development *and* maintenance.

The Top Ten

Boehm's top ten metrics (1987) are:

1. One hundred times more expensive to fix a delivered error than one caught early.
2. Software schedules can only compress by 25 percent (using given methods and tools).
3. Every dollar of development will cost you two for maintenance.
4. Software development and maintenance costs are a function of the number of executable instructions in the product: cost = $f(ELOC)$.
5. Variations between people account for the biggest differences in software productivity.
   Moral: Get the best people working on your project or train everyone to the level of the best.
6. Ratio of software to hardware cost is 85 : 15 and growing.
7. Only 15 percent of software development effort is programming (i.e., coding). Best practices now spend 60 percent of their time on requirements and design, and only 25 percent testing.
8. Software systems and products cost three times as much per instruction as an individual program. System software products (i.e., compilers and operating systems) cost nine times as much.

9. Walkthroughs are the most cost-effective technique for eliminating existing software errors, catching 60 percent of all errors.

10. Software phenomena follow a Pareto distribution:

20 percent of the modules consume 80 percent of the resources

20 percent of the modules contribute 80 percent of the errors

20 percent of the errors consume 80 percent of repair costs

20 percent of the enhancements consume 80 percent of the adaptive maintenance costs

20 percent of the modules consume 80 percent of the execution time

20 percent of the tools experience 80 percent of the tool usage.

IMPLEMENTING MEASUREMENTS

Measurements must be implemented very carefully unless you want to kill the whole project. First, you can and probably should involve the people who will be using the measurements in the process of developing them. Use the rapid evolutionary development process to create the initial set of measurements. Once these are in place, there must be broad, extensive training so that everyone knows what the measurements are and how they can be used to *help improve the process*. Measurements that target and punish workers will kill productivity and quality.

EVALUATING MEASUREMENTS

Use the PDCA process to evaluate the effectiveness of the measurements you do implement. Don't be afraid to toss some out and create new ones. Measurement, like every other process you follow, must grow and evolve if it is to be effective in your environment. Static measurement processes, like any other unchanging activity, are a sure sign of decay.

CONTINUOUS IMPROVEMENT

Measurements have no value and will only burden the company unless you use the seven basic quality improvement tools (described in Chapter 10) to continuously improve all of your processes, products, and people. Attempting to improve processes without measurements is a painful process. You need data about the process to be able to improve it. Thus measurements must precede quality improvement activities by as much as 18 months to enable you to develop a useful base of information.

SUMMARY

Software measurements are vital key on the stairway to software excellence. Without them, evaluating and improving software processes would be impossible.

Software measurements can also be dangerous. If used to measure people instead of processes or tools, they will create havoc in your information systems department.

To adequately begin to measure productivity and quality, we can begin collecting the following measurements and using them to continuously improve the software process:

1. Function points per staff month (upward trend)
2. Noncommentary lines of code per staff month (upward trend)
3. Defects per thousand lines of code (downward trend)
4. Cyclomatic complexity (5–9 per module)

For more information on software measurement, see Arthur (1985) and Grady (1987).

CHAPTER 10

Software Quality

It is not uncommon to find an MIS department with no formal quality program, whose quality costs are 30% or even 50% of the annual MIS budget. This is a very expensive and slow way to build software.

— Richard Zultner (1988)

With the arrival of the information economy, customers have begun to demand software quality. Market demand for quality will drive radical changes in the software industry and this is good. Unfortunately, most ideas of what constitutes software quality are sadly misguided. There are a number of myths about quality:

- Software failures are unavoidable
- Testing delivers quality
- Quality costs money

Current software development processes produce two products: software (code, documentation, and so on) and defects (causing rework, waste, loss of productivity, higher costs).

The cost of finding and removing these defects is 50 percent of all software costs (Brooks 1975). This exorbitant cost has become chronic because *the software process is planned this way.* The current method of finding these defects focuses only on quality control.

Quality has encountered a number of metaphors: quality is free, quality is conformance to valid customer requirements, quality is zero defects, and quality is a journey not a destination. As you will discover, software quality is all of these things and more.

Known software techniques make defect-free software possible. Most software professionals, however, avoid doing all of the things required to achieve zero-defect software. "Too much structure," they proclaim. "Too much bureaucracy."

Most software companies foolishly base all of their defect efforts on finding bugs once they're in the software. Computer testing to identify and remove defects will find at most 70 percent of the defects. The number of defects that slip through testing is a function of the number of defects *in the software when it is delivered for testing*. The number of defects in the software when delivered to testing is a direct function of the quality of the process used to create the software. Testing can only uncover 70 percent of the latent defects in the code. Inspections can remove 80–90 percent of the defects before testing, but a good process will prevent defects from ever entering the product.

There are a few key elements about quality that need to be understood:

- Quality is a market-based strategy. Quality creates and maintains market share, even inside a company.
- Quality is a function of the process used to create a product, whether that product is hardware, software, or that elusive factor—management.
- Quality is customer driven. Customers demand high quality and without it, they won't continue using your service or product. Higher quality results in increased productivity, profits, and market share (Figure 10.1). Higher quality results in lower unit costs and failure costs.
- Quality must be woven into the fabric of the system as it is created. It cannot be tested in.

The key software qualities are:

1. Flexibility for new methods and technologies
2. Extensibility via an open architecture
3. Reusability for optimal productivity
4. Integration via automation
5. Maintainability via design level maintenance and evolution

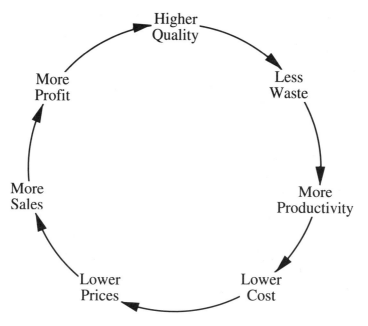

Figure 10.1 The Deming Chain

6. Consistency via data-driven documentation (e.g., repository/encyclopedia)
7. Usability via software pilot training

Within this framework, one meaningful software quality goal is the absence of defects. The only way to assure the absence of defects is to avoid putting them into the product. The only way to avoid putting them in the product is to improve the process to prevent them.

Quality is not just the absence of defects. From the customer's perspective, quality means the presence of value as well as the absence of defects. Customers want long-term value that saves them time, effort, and frustration.

Quality does cost money, but delivering a quality product costs less than delivering a shoddy product. The "invisible" costs of downtime and rework and possible warranty charges vastly outweigh the cost of delivering quality. There are three costs of quality: failure, appraisal, and prevention. Failure costs arise when software fails before or after release. Failures require analysis, debugging, rework, retest, and reinstallation—failure costs. Appraisal costs include the costs of inspecting or testing the software prior to release to find defects. In good companies, this cost is as low as 25 percent of the total cost; in poor companies appraisal costs can run as high as 50 percent. Prevention costs include the costs of training and application of the methods and tools of continuous quality improvement. The company that can deliver quality software in the 1990s will suffer no lack of work or customer disdain. It has been widely rumored that it takes eight times as much investment to get a new customer as it does to keep an old one. Quality keeps them coming back. Quality is:

- A systematic process for continuous improvement, not a function or a department
- Everybody's job, not just a few specialists'
- Applicable to all activities, not just manufacturing
- What the buyer wants and needs, not what suppliers want to provide
- The continuous application of quality improvement techniques, not a periodic quality inquisition
- The foundation for planning, doing, and automating all processes

Quality improvement is not without its problems. What are the pitfalls of quality improvement? Typically, they are a lack of:

- Understanding quality and its benefits at all levels in the organization
- Acceptance of where we are and where we have to go
- Involvement, on a personal level, with quality improvement
- Support for quality improvement (investment, resources, time)
- Expectations, goals, and objectives for quality improvement
- Recognition and reward for success

All of these potential problems revolve around the people that will use the quality improvement and software processes.

PEOPLE

The industrial revolution created a paradigm that people are just factors of production. People are no longer just factors in production; *people are the production* when it comes to software. Technology isn't the barrier to software excellence, change is the barrier. Change only occurs through training that involves the eyes, ears, and bodies of software developers and maintainers and managers.

A major weakness in software lies in the way people cooperate, manage, and organize themselves. Technology isn't the barrier—change is. Often, the goals of developers, customers, project managers, maintainers, operators, and management are in conflict. The winners and the losers of the 1990s will be separated by mentality and attitude, not nationality.

Specialists

Succeeding at rapid evolutionary development will require the creation of specialists:

- User interface
- Data design and database
- Processing (for minimal maintenance and maximum growth)
- System interface
- Documentation
- Training
- Software process evolution
- Measurement and estimation
- Quality

Wouldn't it be great if these specialists already existed? Unfortunately, there are very few Bachs, Beethovens, or Mozarts in the IS community. There is no vast pool of excellent people. Managers must therefore develop these talents in their staff. There is little wonder that the most costly portion of achieving software excellence will be transferring the technology and methodology to the staff.

PROCESS

There never seems to be time to do it right, but customers, managers, and technicians always seem to suggest that there will be time to redo a system. These ridiculous notions waste your most precious commodity—time. There is never time to re-create a poorly built system, but organizations do so. Software, unlike houses or machinery, simply doesn't wear out. Here again, the construction paradigm has gotten us into trouble. In America, we tear down old buildings and put up new ones or we sell our old clunker and buy a new car. There is no reason, however, to replace software. It will run forever given that the hardware can be maintained to support it.

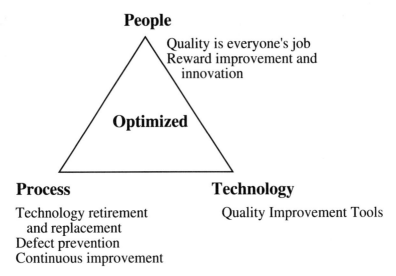

People

Quality is everyone's job
Reward improvement and
  innovation

Optimized

Process

Technology retirement
  and replacement
Defect prevention
Continuous improvement

Technology

Quality Improvement Tools

Figure 10.2   Optimized Process

To succeed at software evolution, prototypers and managers alike must shift from the mistaken belief that you can buy a replacement system. Mass production has us convinced that we can buy replacement products easily and effortlessly. Software, unfortunately, is only produced by custom development (odd isn't it that "custom" is the first portion of "customer").

There is no silver bullet.

— Brooks (1988)

There appear to be two theories about how to improve software quality and productivity. The silver bullet theory focuses on major innovations to improve productivity and quality. Silver bullets are very American, but occur infrequently, for example, miracles. Continuous improvement, however, focuses on slow, steady improvement that incorporates innovations as they arise. It is usually done every day by everyone. It relies on the small win.

IS must learn to create the right systems (the ones of most value) and then to create the systems in the right way (Figure 10.2). We often attain unanimous agreement to create a system, and then develop it in ways that result in a system that none of us wants. The user may not know exactly what they want or what IS can deliver. Consequently short cuts are taken, requirements missed, and objectives overlooked.

In the past, IS departments have depended on their gurus to take them from conception to delivered product. To rise out of chaos into the repeatable and defined steps of software maturity, IS must shift to software processes that are both rapid and effective. IS must focus on preventing defects rather than detecting and correcting them through software testing. Prevention focuses on integrating quality into the software process through planning, evolutionary analysis and design, acquisition of support tools that prevent errors and variation, and training for all developers in new techniques and tools. To prevent errors, there must be a written process for rapid evolutionary development and continuous evolution of the resulting initial system (Arthur 1988).

The first portion of software evolution focuses on software creation that uses a rapid prototyping methodology that emphasizes reuse of data, program components, and parts—the knowledge, organs, and cells of the system. Like matter, which consists of reusable parts—electrons, neutrons, protons, and other subatomic particles—and music, which reuses notes to form compositions, software must do the same. To succeed at software evolution, IS must follow the natural order of the universe and begin to reuse components that consist of smaller software parts or cells. Successful reuse programs begin with pools of data as the knowledge base and evolve to include the various code, modules, programs, and subsystems that process the underlying data into information. Any attempt to begin with processing first will ultimately have to retrace some steps to create the databases necessary for the company to improve and evolve.

The second portion of software evolution focuses on the evolutionary process—software maintenance. Software maintenance structures the customer's change requests and problem reports into scheduled system releases that maximize productivity through grouping changes by interim product—data, program, or documentation—and through the ability to schedule and rigorously test each of these as it is changed. The evolutionary maintenance methodology establishes a way to grow a system from its infancy into adulthood through small, incremental, evolutionary enhancement steps and genetic or surgical repairs. Where maintenance once consumed 80 percent of the IS budget, evolution will consume less than 50 percent, leaving the remainder to deliver new systems and functions via the rapid evolutionary development process.

TECHNOLOGY

Until you pick a methodology for both development and maintenance, you can hardly expect to choose effective tools to automate either. There are some tools, however, that are essential regardless of environment.

Most companies are still mired in the tar pit of chaos. To achieve the next level of the stairway to software excellence—the repeatable stage complete with serious project management control—IS must have a mechanism to manage change to the evolving software system, change and configuration management. Change management tracks requested changes (i.e., nibbles) to the system. Configuration management controls and tracks changes to the actual system components—data, code, and documentation.

Software editors, compilers, debuggers, and so on are all necessary. Electronic communication—E-Mail, voice mail, and video—are all excellent facilities to assist in moving the project forward through the transmission of enormous amounts of information. Wherever possible, video is preferable to voice mail because it carries as close to 100 percent of the human communication channel as possible and voice is preferable to E-mail because it carries almost 50 percent of the human channel, while E-mail carries only 7 percent.

The third level of the stairway to software excellence—a defined process—can be automated through the use of appropriate tools that match the process. At this point, computer-aided software engineering (CASE) tools become useful. Without a proven process, however, they are largely a waste of money. And unless they can mate with other tools, they are largely useless. The key to technology excellence and rapid response is integration, not alienation.

The fourth level—software measurement—is the checking step of the PDCA cycle. IS prototypers and managers must be able to check the process and tools through the use of software metrics if there is to be any hope of improvement. Through measurement, system evolutionists can spot the 20 percent of the system that are generating 80 percent of the costs and determine the actions required to reduce the expense. Re-engineering and restructuring tools will automate most of the genetic re-engineering required to bring the data or code back into balance with the rest of the system. These tools can improve productivity and quality by 10–35 percent. Through measurement, a prototyper can also tell if an evolving data structure or a module of code are growing too large to be maintained by mere mortals. Measurement helps you know where you are compared to your own history. Comparing yourself to others, however, is a sure method for an early suicide.

Testing tools will continue to be important means to check a product, but will begin to fade away as they become a waste of resources. At Fujitsu in Japan, systems developers have eliminated the final system test because it no longer discovers enough bugs to be cost effective. Fujitsu has a measured defect rate of ten defects per million lines of code. This is lower than the space shuttle (at 70 defects per million lines) and two orders of magnitude better than typical software (at 2,000–3,000 defects per million lines).

The fifth and highest level of software excellence applies the seven basic quality improvement tools and the other seven advanced tools offer the implements necessary to solve almost any process problem an IS department will ever uncover. These tools are easily created manually and there are numerous tools to help the apprentice quality improvement person automate the development of pareto charts, scatter diagrams, histograms, and similar graphics.

Seven basic tools drive the quality revolution—flowcharts, checksheets, pareto diagrams, cause and effect diagrams, histograms, scatter diagrams, and control charts. For the next few pages we will look at a few that can dramatically improve your customer's perception of the system even before the first design is drawn or the first line of code compiled. We accomplish this shift by turning our emphasis to the user's processes and using the quality tools to tune the process first, then automate it.

USER PROCESSES

Automation is very effective in helping us do the things we already know how to do well. It is not effective, however, in helping us do things in the most effective and efficient manner unless we are already doing them well. Effective user processes must precede the automation of systems. Otherwise, creating an application will only trap the user in unproductive methods of behavior for years to come.

If you just automate the existing process, you are doing a disservice to your customer. The best way to help your customers is to begin by drawing a picture of their process using a structured flowchart. Making and using flowcharts is essential to understanding, simplifying, and automating customers' processes.

As you read this, some of you may be as skeptical as I was when originally exposed to this concept. After all, we abandoned flowcharts as a design tool years ago. They've long since been replaced by data flow and entity relationship diagrams. What's all this stuff about flowcharts?

Well, flowcharts are not the best program design tool, but they can easily diagram a user's process in such a way that:

1. You can understand it
2. You can identify how to simplify it *before* you automate it

Begin by involving the user, their customers and suppliers. All members must contribute to the development of the flowchart. Keep the evolving flowchart visible to everyone at all times. Encourage questions; they are the life blood of getting a well-defined process. Use the meta-model questions described in Chapter 4 to illuminate issues such as:

- Who makes the decision?
- Who supplies what to whom?
- When does each process occur?
- What would happen if . . . (we did something else)?
- What stops us from doing it a different way?
- Where does the product go?

The only question to avoid is the "why" question, which invariably throws people into an endless loop of telling war stories and taking unproductive side trips.

By involving the people who actually perform the process, they gain a sense of control over it. Once this feeling is established, they often feel open to making changes in the process. Once they have described the process, they can also begin to identify useful improvements. A well-diagrammed process assists users and their customers and suppliers in knowing their roles. It also improves communication among all parties and gets you, the system creator, an inside track on understanding their real needs. The resulting flowchart often serves as useful documentation for requirements and training.

At the highest level (Figure 10.3), you need to know the user's *customers* and *suppliers*. Then you can begin to break down the user's internal process (Figure 10.4). What often happens, as in this example, is that one group is responsible for catching another group's errors. By making suppliers (i.e., the employees) responsible for catching their errors *before* sending in their time sheets, payroll errors and delays can be kept to a minimum (Figure 10.5).

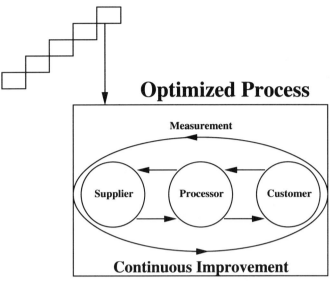

Figure 10.3   Customer-Supplier Model

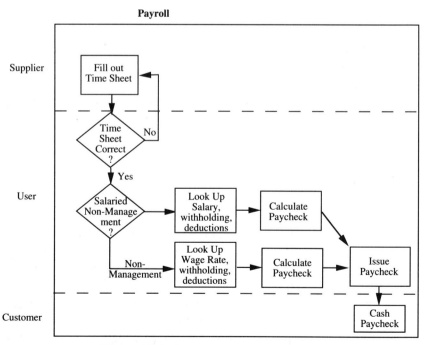

Figure 10.4   Payroll Process Example

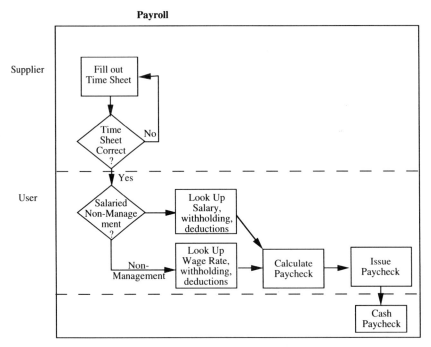

Figure 10.5   Revised Payroll Process

In other cases, there will be complex feedback loops that can be simplified and whole steps that can be eliminated. Simplifying their process will help you simplify the actual creation of the system. It also helps your customer understand their requirements better before you begin the rapid evolutionary development process.

INSPECTIONS

Appraisal (or checking) software quality involves inspection, auditing, testing, and tracking and resolving errors. Most IS departments squander their budget on testing the code, completely ignoring the other more important aspects of the process. Prevention and appraisal activities are *most effective early in the software life cycle*. "By increasing prevention activities significantly and by doing appraisal activities more efficiently, total quality costs can be cut in half within two to three years" (Zultner 1988). No organization can afford to pay its IS staff to create and then correct software defects.

A defect is an instance in which a requirement is not satisfied.
                                            — Michael Fagan (1986)

Once an analyst or a programmer has planned and created a product, inspections serve as a way to check for defects and to act to improve the product. Inspections can save 9–25 percent of development expense (Fagan 1986) because defects are found before they multiply and spread. Inspections also minimize the number of defects that escape the testing process, thereby minimizing costly downtime and rework with delivered systems.

The inspection process uses the PDCA cycle as well, but not just to improve the product. Measurements are the key output of the inspection process. They provide the data on how to improve the process to prevent defects from occurring.

The Inspection Process

Plan	Select materials, participants, and roles
	Learn the material under review
Do	Find defects
	Discourage solving the defects, just find them
	Having checked the product, the author acts to correct the identified defects
	Classify and record the type of defects found
Check	Follow up to ensure all corrections and to prevent the injection of new defects
	Evaluate the types and numbers of defects found
Act	Improve the process that created the defects using defect analysis
	Improve the inspection process to catch more of the common defect types

CRITICAL SUCCESS FACTORS

There are three key leverage points for improving productivity and quality: people, process, and tools. The emphasis to date has been on technology— CASE—to provide the mystical silver bullet. Without a balanced focus on people and the process, however, quality and productivity cannot be achieved. The key to quality is the process or methodology; yet people and technology play their parts. To maximize quality and productivity, we need to *begin* with a defined process and then implement the measurements and data collection required to move to the continuous quality improvement. Using the SEI Software Maturity Framework, we can identify the following critical success factors for each step on the stairway to software excellence and software quality:

Repeatable Process

1. Establish a software quality assurance group to implement quality management
2. Establish *software configuration control/management* for each project
3. Establish *formal procedures* for software engineers to:
   a. Make estimates of software size
   b. Produce software schedules
   c. Estimate software costs
4. Measure and gather statistics of:
   a. *Software size* for each software configuration item, over time
   b. *Defects,* from requirements through production
5. Establish a *change management mechanism* for software engineers to control changes to the software—requirements, design, code, documentation, and so on
6. Establish a *formal procedure* for management to review software projects
7. Establish a *formal procedure* for software testing

Defined Process

1. Develop a *standardized* and *documented* software development/maintenance *process* for each project
2. Establish a software engineering *process group* to evolve the development and maintenance process
3. Develop a required software engineering training program for software professionals
4. Establish a formal training program required for *design and code inspections*
5. Conduct internal software design and code inspections

6. Track the action items resulting from design and code inspections
7. Establish a *mechanism* to ensure compliance with the software engineering *standards*
8. Establish a *mechanism* for assuring the adequacy of regression testing

Managed Process

1. Establish a *mechanism* used for the introduction of new technologies
2. Estimate design, code, and test defects and compare them to actuals
3. Measure *software defects* and record them for each phase of testing and operation
4. Establish a *process database* for *process metrics* data across all projects
5. Analyze the defect data from inspections and tests to determine where to improve the process; conduct analyses of defects to determine their *process* related causes
6. Establish a *mechanism* for periodically assessing the software engineering *process* and implementing indicated improvements

Optimized Process

1. Establish a *mechanism* for identifying and replacing obsolete technologies
2. Establish a *mechanism* for initiating defect prevention actions
3. Establish a *mechanism* for rewarding continuous improvement and innovation

TOOLS AND TECHNOLOGY

Tools and technology are used to support the development and maintenance processes, not as an end in themselves. As previously stated, an organization must have achieved a defined process to be able to make use of CASE technology. The critical components of a successful, productive, high-quality software technology environment are:

1. Automated configuration and change management to control and track change activity throughout the software process
2. Reusable data, code, and documentation

3. High-order languages
4. Tools:
   a. Design and documentation facilities—25 percent of project costs are documentation
   b. Electronic communication facilities—E-mail, conferencing, voice, and so on
   c. Change management
   d. Configuration management
   e. Editors
   f. Compilers
   g. Interactive testing tools

The most common failing of any IS department has been the wholesale introduction of CASE tools or methods without proper training to enable the IS staff to use them effectively. Very few people have the curiosity to open up a new tool, dive in, and swim around for a while to learn how to use it. If the tool isn't intuitively obvious, most people will just abandon it and move back to the way they know that works and then IS management wonders why they haven't received the big bang the vendor suggested would be forthcoming from the implementation of this new tool kit. Small wonder.

One bad experience with a new CASE tool can sour a department's taste for new tools as well, especially when there is no methodology framework to hang it on. IS staff spot a new disaster forming quickly and move to the side to watch the fireworks.

There are four key learning styles: *doers* who just try things, *reviewers* who read all about it, *theorists* who just want the concepts, and *pragmatics* who want real life problems and subjects. Any IS environment consists of mainly people who have some background in software. Unfortunately, this means that any training will usually require a period of *unlearning* because it is impossible for people to learn what they think they already know. They must first unlearn before they can relearn.

ORGANIZING FOR QUALITY AND PRODUCTIVITY

To maximize productivity and quality, we will need to reduce the causes of poor quality: *procedures and methods, materials, environment, people,* and *external factors.*

First, we'll need a process for working effectively, then we'll need tools that automate as much of that method as possible. We will need to train our developers and maintainers in the use of these methods and tools. Then we'll need a culture that rewards high quality and productivity. And finally, we will need measurements to determine if we are working effectively. This implies that we need five organizations:

- **An executive software quality council** *that supports high-quality software development and maintenance. This will help ensure that we move constantly toward the top 5 percent of all software companies.*

- **A process/methodology group** that continuously improves development and maintenance methodologies. The group works closely with the quality management and measurement groups. The 10:1 difference in organizations is partially a reflection of the process used to develop and maintain software. Attention focused on this key element will maximize quality and productivity.

- **A training council** to ensure that training stays abreast of our processes and technology. In this way, we can maximize the quality and productivity of each person by keeping the differences between individuals well below a ratio of 10:1.

- **A measurements council** that collects and continuously refines productivity and quality measurements in support of continuous quality improvement. Without measurement, we cannot understand the impact of changes in technology, methodology, or culture. Using the Hewlett-Packard model for implementing a companywide software measurement program (Grady 1988), form a software metrics council, which will choose the initial set of productivity and quality measurements. Then manage the data collected. A metrics database will be required to facilitate analysis. The metrics council will update the measurements as required to meet the needs of the process organization.

  Train everyone in the application of the initial set of measurements.

- **A culture/sociology/environment council** that uses the law of cause and effect to examine the results achieved and the environmental causes. The other half of the 10:1 difference between organizations is a *quality* culture.

Process/Methodology

Why do you need a process group? Simple: A recent study (Hopcroft & Kraft 1987) found that of the $255 billion spent on software in the United States, $100 billion was for debugging—defect removal. It typically costs three times as much to debug a program as it did to write it. And an estimated 60 percent of all enhancements correct *specification* bugs. Specification bugs also create the need for the replacement of existing systems. The current methods of software development and maintenance have created a *debugging industry*. The cost of poor quality is $100 billion for not doing it right the first time.

Deming (1986) states that the cost of poor quality in U.S. industries is 25–40 percent of total expense. The $100 billion figure puts software at the high end of this scale. "Well it's always been that way!" But companies with an emphasis on quality processes have found that they can achieve rates of 5 percent or less, *saving 20–35 percent of their total expense.* Would this make you more competitive? More testing isn't the answer.

If we had a report program that produced pages of defects, would you hire a staff of cutters and pasters to fix it? Unlikely—you'd fix the program. You probably have a development process that produces software loaded with defects (1–3 defects per 1,000 LOC). Instead of fixing the process, testers, debuggers, and maintainers to cut, paste, and patch the product are hired. Which would you rather pay for, someone to put in the defects and take them out again, or someone to fix the process to prevent defects?

In the best companies, quality is the rule! Ignoring the process is a recipe for *minimizing* quality and productivity.

Training

To keep your corporation and employees ahead of the competition, you need to invest in employee quality through continuous training and retraining. Capers Jones (1987) has examined the data from thousands of corporations and the leading-edge companies have 15 or more days per year of training for every employee. Peters (1987) says the same thing. To be the best, we will need a training council to ensure excellence.

Measurement

"You can't manage what you can't measure!"
— Tom DeMarco (1982)

This is a basic engineering principle. And anything you're not measuring is getting worse. There are some excellent metrics of productivity and quality that have been validated over the years. But to be useful, they must be analyzed and *calibrated* to reflect your culture and environment. A measurement group can make this happen.

Culture/Sociology/Environment

Some organizations are more productive than others by an order of magnitude (10:1). We know from measurements that Hitachi and Toshiba have a 6:1 advantage over most other companies. We are all using similar tools and similar methods. Something has to be different, and that something is culture. If you look at U.S. culture, we reward: the quick fix, hot, high tech, new projects, and firefighting. However, we rarely recognize or reward: continuous improvement, teamwork, process and cultural improvements, teams that deliver on time and within schedule, teams that re-engineer their systems to reduce maintenance costs, and fire prevention.

The results we're achieving from a faulty process that produces defect-ridden software are the direct result of our recognition and reward systems. To achieve high productivity and quality (because without quality, high productivity doesn't matter), we must change the way we recognize and reward employees.

The most important finding of DeMarco's (1985) and Boehm's (1987) studies is that in order to maximize productivity and quality, employees need 100 sq. ft. of *enclosed*, private workspace, with 30 sq. ft. of desk area. This flies in the face of the furniture police and the blitzkrieg advertising of the nation's furniture vendors, but it is has been studied and confirmed. In an open office cubicle, average workers are interrupted every 11 minutes. This prevents them from achieving the *flow* necessary to productive work. In the best companies, workers achieved 2–3 *hours* of flow in enclosed spaces as compared to 0–1 in the worst. The difference in performance is at least 3:1.

This, the authors contend, is a cultural issue based on short-sighted, next-quarter thinking. The additional cost of enclosed space is about $1,300/person to achieve a return of 3:1 on the total cost for the employee—salary, benefits, and so forth.

What about the Japanese, some people ask? They work on narrow tables, scrunched together. True! In a discussion with DeMarco, however, the head engineer of Hitachi told him that if they could solve their space problems, especially in Tokyo, they would *bury* the U.S. software industry.

Can we afford to sink tens of thousands of dollars into hardware for each programmer and then leave them open to a nonproductive environment for the lack of a few thousand dollars worth of walls and doors? Or should we make it easier on the furniture police when they need to change arrangements? In 1979, when I first implemented UNIX, a terminal on every desk was considered a ridiculous expense. Time and measurement have shown that workstations are an essential part of quality and productivity for the software professional; enclosed workspaces are no less important.

A cultural/sociological organization is needed in order to see these changes. If culture is the overriding characteristic of the 10:1 companies, we need to see that our culture remains in the spotlight for many years to come.

Culture/Sociology/Environment

These kinds of far-reaching opportunities have traditionally been handled by management between budget views. They are best handled by quality teams, by putting the power back in the hands of the software professional. From this standpoint the issue of cultural change is best addressed by the process group.

Estimating

DeMarco (1982) recommended that estimating be handled by one group. Here again, specialization would encourage excellence. Estimators can be measured on the accuracy of their estimate. Setting unrealistic dates and sacrificing quality for expediency will cause you to pay the price in terms of long-range maintenance costs. Accurate estimates can help resolve this problem. Productivity metrics that include both development and maintenance costs will further reduce this problem.

SOFTWARE QUALITY AND PRODUCTIVITY IMPROVEMENT METHODOLOGY

The critical success factor of high-quality and productivity organizations is a method to continuously introduce improvements in their processes. This can be accomplished through the use of the quality improvement process and the implementation of a methodology to accomplish these goals.

This process or methodology consists of five iterative steps, which loosely follow the PDCA process:

1. Assessing the present software process maturity
2. Analyzing the results of the assessment to determine priorities
3. Setting goals for improvement
4. Implementing the improvements
5. Measuring the impact of the improvements (see Chapter 9)

Assessing Software Process Maturity

The software assessment process uses the software process maturity framework (Humphrey 1989) questionnaires to determine the maturity of a development or maintenance process. As we learn more about our software processes, this questionnaire will evolve to support the refinements necessary to achieve software excellence.

Analyzing the Assessment

Once the data has been collected and processed, a report will need to be issued that identifies key strengths and opportunities for improvement. Based on this report, the assessed project should perform the following steps:

1. Form a team of technicians to analyze the report
2. Prioritize the critical success action items according to project needs
3. Identify:
    a. What can be changed
    b. What must be changed by working through others
4. Set objectives to implement a reasonable set of these items
5. Brainstorm solutions
    a. Identify resources required (including other groups)
    b. Identify the costs
    c. Identify any roadblocks (and a plan to overcome them one at a time)
    d. Identify the risks associated with each change
6. Create a plan for implementation of these goals during the coming year

Format for an Assessment Response

Each assessment will need to identify the following:

1. The level of process maturity
2. Strengths
3. Opportunities for improvement
4. Goal for improvements in:
    a. Critical success factors
    b. Tools
    c. Methods
    d. Environment

Once the assessment is complete, the time has come for planning the changes and resources required, implementing the change, and using measurement to check the results. Software assessment is yet another form of PDCA that can be used to vault your company toward excellence.

PDCA

The PDCA process uses three main tools to solve 80 percent of all quality problems: checksheets, pareto charts, and Ishikawa (or fishbone) diagrams. Checksheets (Figure 10.6) help the prototyper gather data about the software creation and evolution process. Pareto charts (Figure 10.7) help the prototyper identify the *vital few* problems as opposed to the *trivial*

	Module 1	Module 2	Module 3	Total
Total Defects	||	ЦЖ ЦЖ ЦЖ ЦЖ ||||	|	27
	2	24	1	27

Figure 10.6 Defects by Module Checksheet

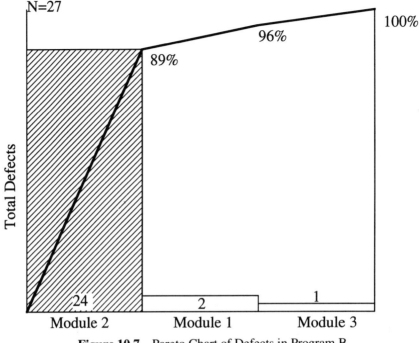

Figure 10.7   Pareto Chart of Defects in Program B

many. Then the prototyper can use the Ishikawa diagram (Figure 10.8) to identify the *root causes* of the problems they've experienced. From this, the prototyper can begin to identify how to evolve the product or process to eliminate quality problems.

Understanding quality improvement is not a one chapter experience. There are more quality improvement techniques and tools out there than you can possibly imagine, but learning to use these three will benefit every aspect of your software process.

Training for Quality

> *Total Quality Control starts with training and ends with training. To implement TQC, we need to carry out continuous education for everyone, from the president down to line workers.*
>
> *— Kaoru Ishikawa*

Empowering employees to solve the problems of the business is the second largest investment IS will ever make and the best one as well. Most of the companies that go after the Malcolm Baldrige award spend a minimum of

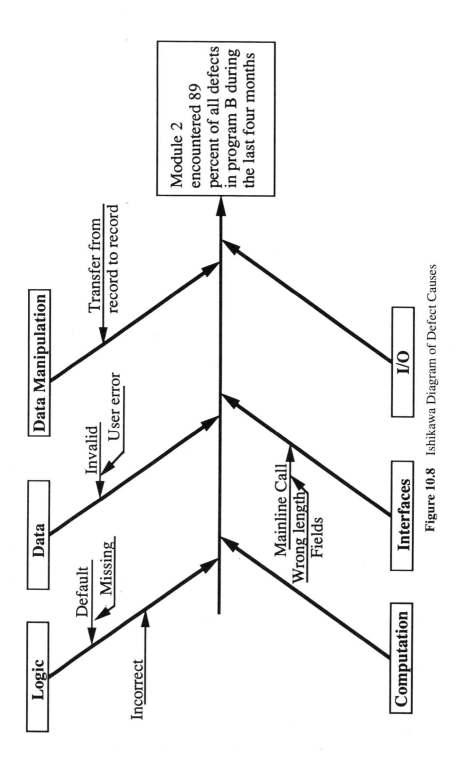

Figure 10.8 Ishikawa Diagram of Defect Causes

four days and about $1,400 per person to train employees in the use of the quality improvement process. Motorola has found that quality training delivers a 33:1 return on investment (Moskal 1990). Every Motorola employee must take a minimum of 40 hours of training each year. Every Motorola department spends 2.4–2.8 percent of its budget on training and Motorola expects to double the amount of training by 1995 to sustain competitive advantage.

The half-life of the knowledge of a new engineer is about five years.
— Gary Tooker

Quality improvement is a management revolution, but it is not new. In 1950, Deming took quality improvement techniques to Japan. The techniques were invented about 30 years earlier. Now, in the 1990s, Japanese quality is highly regarded in many fields of endeavor. The 1990s will see an explosion in quality training as companies struggle to compete in the global village for a piece of the ever-expanding market. Unfortunately, much of this training will be focused on manufacturing and not on software—the black art. The Japanese, although trailing in software technology, have made great strides in using quality techniques on software. If the past is any indication, they will be a formidable software opponent in this decade.

No matter how hard Western nations try to engage in QC education, they may not catch up with Japan until the 1990s, since it requires ten years for the QC education to take effect.
— J. M. Juran (1987)

Every level in an organization needs a minimum of five days of quality training. Executives will require a slightly different approach than employees. Software developers will need custom training that will be somewhat different from that required by maintainers or operations. Training must begin at the top and then cascade down through the hierarchy. Once companies complete entry level training in quality improvement, the training continues. "QC education has been conducted in Japan since 1949 without interruption" (Ishikawa 1985). "Formal education is less than one-third of the total educational effort. It is the responsibility of the boss to teach his subordinates through actual work." A behavioral example from a peer or a supervisor is worth a week of classroom training.

Companies that attempt to leap over the other developmental stages of software maturity to the highest level will experience significant pain and expense. To begin quality improvement, you must have the data that comes from measurements. To measure correctly, you must have a defined process with supporting tools. To have either of these, you need some basic project controls in place. Like human development, each stage, from infancy to childhood to adolescence to adulthood must be experienced. Companies can't jump from infancy to adulthood; they must grow and evolve toward excellence. Throughout this evolution, training and education will assure the rapid growth of productivity and quality.

SUMMARY

To maximize both quality and productivity during software creation and evolution you will need to:

- Apply the quality improvement process including *assessment* for gathering data about our current sophistication and *measurement* to evaluate our progress
- Organize for quality
- Expand your training commitment
- Create an optimum environment for software work that includes and rewards excellence in both development and maintenance

Through the application of assessment, measurement, training, and the quality improvement process, you can expect to be in the top 5 percent in 5–10 years. Without this investment in continuous improvement, there is every likelihood that a competitor will overrun you before the turn of the century.

Recommendations for Action

In his book, *Planning for Quality* (1987), J. M. Juran identifies the "Quality Trilogy":

Quality planning	Planning for quality (management's job)
Quality management	Defect *prevention* and continuous improvement
Quality control	Defect *detection* and removal

To begin to achieve quality, we must address each of these three key elements.

1. We must commit to developing quality awareness and skills in all of our personnel
   a. All quality improvements begin with training
   b. All managers must attend *Quality* education and begin planning for total quality management (TQM). To succeed at quality requires leadership.
   c. The technical staff need training in:
      i. Quality management: quality awareness—familiarity with quality management; quality project team training—for specific quality teams; and quality consultant training—for quality consultants
      ii. Quality control—inspections and testing
2. We must commit to quality management—the *prevention* of defects
   a. We must develop methods and tools for defect prevention and continuous improvement. We need to implement a quality improvement process to:
      i. Identify improvements in our management and technical processes
      ii. Implement those improvements to: prevent defects; reduce costs; and increase productivity and quality
      iii. Implement measurements to evaluate the effectiveness of improvements
3. We must intensify our existing commitment to quality control. Inspections should be required for all work products—requirements, designs, code, test cases, user documentation, and so forth. Since computer testing alone is only 70 percent efficient (leaving 30 percent of the bugs in the code), inspections of all work products are essential to raise defect removal efficiency to 95 percent (Capers Jones)
4. We must establish a group that continuously implements and improves quality
   a. It is not possible to make one group responsible for quality, but it is possible to create a group which *is* responsible for implementing the quality trilogy: quality planning, quality control, and quality management. These three processes are the keys to high productivity and dramatically reduced costs
   b. Quality is a low-risk investment that pays huge dividends

5. Training requirements
   a. Maximize effectiveness; to maximize effectiveness, training must be:
      i. Delivered when needed—just in time training
      ii. About a problem the participant needs to resolve, not some artificial one
      iii. Flexible to leverage existing knowledge (e.g., how is object oriented programming like structured programming?)
   b. Maximize return on investment (ROI); to maximize ROI, training must:
      i. Increase a participant's skills by at least an order of magnitude
      ii. Ensure that the participant retains these skills
      iii. Deliver a solution to an existing business problem
   c. Minimize time away from the office; training needs to be done on an "outpatient" basis; this will require the participant to:
      i. Do some precourse work—reading, problem selection, video, whatever
      ii. Attend the training (initially instructor led, trending to CAI/Interactive video with an AI copilot)
      iii. Complete the course by resolving the business problem they've prepared
      iv. Document and share their success
      v. Feedback into the training curriculum to improve the existing course

Quality

Finally, you must have a team of *quality crazies* working to instill quality in everyone and everything. The typical organization without quality uses 25–40 percent of its expenses on the waste caused by poor quality. Best companies can cut this to 5 percent. You want to cut costs? Quality offers you the way. You want to increase revenues? Quality is also the way.

These ideas are not new, but in our flutter from one silver bullet to the next, in our search for a savior or a magic wand, we have overlooked the obvious or pooh-poohed them as too simple. We must become more like the tortoise and less like the hare; we must seek for continuous progress toward our goal. Then, in our journey, if we run across a silver bullet or a magic wand, we'll know what to do with it.

To climb to the top of the stairway to software excellence, we must implement the following key elements of people, process, and technology:

People	We must establish several key specialist groups:
	Quality improvement specialists—to get quality rolling
	A process team—to improve our processes
	A re-engineering team—to continuously improve all of our software
	A measurement team—to see how we're doing
	An estimating team—to improve our estimates
Process	We need:
	A flexible development methodology
	A defined maintenance methodology
	These methods must be continuously improved to reduce our time-to-market for applications, products, and services.
Technology	We need:
	A full-blown maintenance workbench including re-engineering tools
	A fully integrated development workbench that supports the methodology
	A change management system
	A suite of measurement tools

This is not to say that these efforts are not underway in one form or another throughout software organizations, but they have little common direction and are often derailed by the needs of special interests. Again, we need an inspiring vision, the commitment, and the resources to get there. It will not be cheap, but it will be worth it.

Rapid evolutionary development is not a panacea. It is an evolutionary step on the path toward software excellence. It relies on many existing methods and tools, from communication skills to quality improvement, to ensure its success. Fortunately, these skills give it the ability to adapt to its environment and learn from its mistakes. May you be surprised and delighted by how quickly rapid evolutionary development leads you to new heights of software creation and evolution.

Bibliography

Akima, Noboru and Fusatake Ooi, *Industrializing Software Development: A Japanese Approach*, IEEE Software, March 1989.

Appleton, Daniel S., "Data-Driven Prototyping," *Datamation,* November 1983.

Arthur, Lowell Jay, *Measuring Programmer Productivity and Software Quality,* Wiley, 1985.

Arthur, Lowell Jay, *Software Evolution—The Software Maintenance Challenge,* Wiley, 1988.

Arthur, Lowell Jay, UNIX Shell Programming, 2nd ed., Wiley, 1990.

Bateson, Gregory, Mind and Nature, Bantam, 1979.

Bateson, Gregory and Mary Catherine Bateson, *Angels Fear*, Bantam, 1987.

Belady, L.A. and M.M. Lehman, "A model of large program development," *IBM System Journal,* no. 3, 1976, pp. 225–52.

Bell, C. Gordon, "The fewer engineers per project, the better," IEEE Spectrum, February 1989.

Biggerstaff, Ted J., Design Recovery for Maintenance and Reuse, IEEE Computer, July 1989, pp. 36–49.

Bliss, Edwin C., Doing It Now, Bantam, 1983.

Boehm, Barry, "Industrial software metrics top 10 list," IEEE Software, September 1987.

Brooks, Frederick, *The Mythical Man Month*, Addison-Wesley, 1975.

Brooks, Frederick, "No Silver Bullet," IEEE Software, 1988.

Clason, George S., *The Richest Man in Babylon*, Signet, 1955.

Cobb, Richard H. and Harlan D. Mills, ''Engineering Software under Statistical Quality Control,'' IEEE Software, November 1990.

Covey, Steven R., *The Seven Habits of Highly Effective People*, Simon & Schuster, 1989.

Cox, Brad, ''Planning the Software Industrial Revolution,'' IEEE Software, November 1990.

Cureton, Bill, ''The Future of Unix in the CASE Renaissance,'' IEEE Software, March 1988.

Cusumano, Michael A., *The Software Factory: A Historical Interpretation*, IEEE Software, March 1989.

Davis, Alan M. et al., A Strategy for Comparing Alternative Software Development Life Cycle Models, IEEE Trans. Soft. Eng., vol. 14, no. 10, October 1988.

DeMarco, Tom, Controlling Software Projects, Prentice Hall, 1982.

DeMarco, Tom, ''Software Development: State of the Art vs. State of the Practice,'' ACM Sigsoft, 1989.

DeMarco, Tom, *Making a Difference in the Schools*, IEEE Software, November 1990.

DeMarco, Tom and Tim Lister, ''Programmer Performance and the Effects on the Workplace,'' Proceedings of the 8th International Conference on Software Engineering, IEEE, 1985, pp. 268–72.

Deming, W. Edwards, Out of the Crisis, MIT Press, 1986.

Drucker, Peter E., *Innovation and Entrepreneurship*, Harper & Row, 1986.

Ernst & Young, ''The Landmark MIT Study: Management in the 1990s,'' Ernst & Young, 1989.

Fagan, Michael E., ''Advances in Software Inspections,'' IEEE Trans. on Soft. Eng., SE-12(7), July 1986, pp. 744–51.

Gaffney, ''Estimating the Number of Faults in Code,'' IEEE Trans. on Soft. Eng., SE-10(4), July 1984.

Grady and Caswell, Establishing a company-wide metrics program, Prentice Hall, 1988.

Gross, Neil, ''Now Software Isn't Safe from Japan,'' *Business Week,* February 11, 1991, pg. 84.

Gruman, Galen ed., Early reuse practice lives up to its promise, IEEE Software, November 1988.

Guaspari, John, *I Know It When I See It*, AMA, 1985.

Heider, John, *The Tao of Leadership*, Bantam, 1985.

Hekmatpour, Sharam, ''Experience with Evolutionary Prototyping in a Large Software Project,'' ACM SIGSOFT Eng. Notes, vol. 12, no. 1, January 1987.

Hix, Deborah, *Generations of User-Interface Management Systems*, IEEE Software, September 1990.

Hopcroft and Craft, The Debugging Industry, IEEE Spectrum, December 1987.

Humphrey, Watts S., *Characterizing the Software Process: A Maturity Framework*, IEEE Software, March 1988.

Humphrey, Watts S., *Managing the Software Process*, Addison-Wesley, 1989.

Humphrey, Watts S. and D.H. Kitson, *Preliminary report on conducting SEI-Assisted Assessments of Software Engineering Capability,* Tech. Report, SEI-87-TR-16, Software Eng. Inst., July 1987.

IEEE, Proceedings of the 9th International Conference on Software Engineering, 1987.

International Technophobia, Inc. Magazine, February 1991, p. 77.

John-Roger and Peter McWilliams, *Life 101*, Prelude Press, 1990.

Jones, Capers, Programmer Productivity, Prentice-Hall, 1987.

Juran, Joseph M., Planning for Quality, ASQC, 1987.

Kraushaar, James and L. Shirland, ''Prototyping Information Systems on Micro-computers: A Design Philosophy for Engineering Management,'' Engineering Management International, vol. 3, 1985, pp. 73–84.

Kuhn, T., *The Structure of Scientific Revolutions*, University of Chicago Press, 1962.

Laborde, Genie Z., *Influencing with Integrity*, Syntony, 1984.

Laborde, Genie Z., *90 Days to Communication Excellence*, Syntony, 1985.

Lakoff, George and Mark Johnson, Metaphors We Live By, University of Chicago Press, 1980.

Lewis, Ted G. and Paul W. Oman, The Challenge of Software Development, IEEE Software, November 1990.

Lind, Randy K. and K. Vairavan, ''An Experimental Investigation of Software Metrics and Their Relationship to Software Development Effort,'' IEEE Trans. on Soft. Eng., vol. 15, no. 5, May 1989.

Luqi, ''Software Evolution Through Rapid Prototyping,'' IEEE Computer, May 1989.

Martin, James and Carma McClure, Software Maintenance, Prentice Hall, 1983.

McCabe, T. J., ''A complexity measure,'' IEEE Trans. Soft. Eng., vol. 2, no. 4, pp. 308–20, December 1976.

McEachron, Norman B. and H.S. Javitz, *Quality in Research and Development*, SRI International, Report No. 750, 1987.

Miller, George A., ''The Magical Number Seven, Plus or Minus Two: Some limits on our capacity for Processing Information,'' *Psychological Review,* vol. 63, no. 2, March 1956.

Miller, James Grier, *Living Systems*, McGraw Hill, 1978.

Mills, Harlan D., Michael Dyer, and Richard C. Linger, *Cleanroom Software Engineering*, IEEE Software, September 1987.

Misra, Santosh K. and Paul J. Jalics, *Third-Generation versus Fourth-Generation Software Development*, IEEE Software, 1988.

Moad, Jeff, ''The Software Revolution,'' *Datamation,* February 15, 1990, pp. 22–30.

Moskal, Brian S., "Just a Degree of Confidence," *Industry Week,* February 19, 1990, pp. 65–66.

Parnas, David L., Paul C. Clements, and David M. Weiss, "The Modular Structure of Complex Systems," IEEE Trans. Soft. Eng., SE-11, vol. 3, March 1985, pp. 259–66.

Peters, Tom, Thriving on Chaos, Knopf, 1987.

Peters, Tom, "Do it badly, do it quickly, make it better, and then say you planned it," *Rocky Mountain News*, December 4, 1990, p. B14.

Potosnak, Kathleen, Modular implementation benefits developers, users, IEEE Software, May 1989.

Prieto-Diaz, Ruben and P. Freeman, Classifying Software for Reuse, IEEE Software, January 1987.

Rockart, John F. and David W. DeLong, *Executive Support Systems*, Dow Jones-Irwin, 1988.

Ross, Niall, *Using metrics in quality management*, IEEE Software, July 1990.

Royce, W.W., "Managing the Development of Large Software Systems: Concepts and Techniques," Proceedings, WESCON, August 1970.

Shaw, Mary, Prospects for an Engineering Discipline of Software, IEEE Software, November 1990.

Shmucker, K.J., "MacApp: An Application Framework," *Byte,* August 1986.

Thomas, Lewis, *The Lives of a Cell*, Bantam, 1975.

Withrow, Carol, "Error Density and Size in Ada Software," IEEE Software, January 1990.

Zultner, Richard, "The Deming Approach to Software Quality Engineering," Quality Progress, November 1988.

INDEX